Foreword

Rejoice! How to Find and Keep the Savior's Joy, authored by Fran C. Hafen, is a remarkable book.

During the past several weeks I have read the treasured manuscript three times. The first time because Fran asked me to. The second time because I desired to better understand the message. And the third time because my heart needed to hear these truths again.

The message of this book is gently overwhelming. The glorious ideas expressed will probably not change your life, but will certainly change your heart. All that is happening to you now will continue to happen after you close these pages; however the joy you seek as you move forward will be more reachable, more noticeable, more frequent, more deep, and will flavor your every quiet moment.

I want many things from the smorgasbord of life. However basically, I'm a "Joy Seeker." And Fran, through her disciplined study, her prayerful inspired analysis, her tender heart has fitted me with glasses to find and embrace the very essence of joy.

Obviously Fran has spent innumerable hours searching for, finding, pondering, and organizing the most inspired ideas ever expressed on the subject of joy. She has laid a doctrinal foundation upon which each of us can experience a close and personal relationship with joy.

Using quotes from the "best books" and her inspired mind, this brilliant author has focused our eyes and hearts on joy. She has truly done her homework. However, it is the "home work" she has done with herself, her family, her associates, her Savior, and the Holy Spirit that forms the parts of the book that touched me most.

Thank you Sister Hafen for this treasure.

George Durrant

Introduction: A Prescribed Pathway to Joy

For years, we have heard that we are to find joy in the journey of mortality, but like many Latter-day Saints, my husband and I were a bit surprised when President Russell M. Nelson named joy as a "principle that is key to our spiritual survival." He reminded us that the answer to Lehi's "opposition, anxiety, heartache, pain, disappointment, and sorrow" was simply, "Men are, that they might have joy" (2 Nephi 2:25). Surely, we want to feel happiness and joy, but can seeking and experiencing joy really make a difference in the perils and confusion of the last days? For President Nelson, "the answer is a resounding yes!" In fact, joy is the very "nature and purpose of our lives here in mortality."[1]

The world's definition of joy is merely "a state of happiness or felicity" or "the emotion evoked by well-being, success, or good fortune or by the prospect of possessing what one desires."[2] The problem with such a broad explanation is that all strong feelings of gladness or pleasure then become equally acceptable and that any action leading to one's sense of joy is justifiable based on cultural relativism. No wonder mortals continue to search for joy through money and materialism, power and position, and vanity and even vice! This is why President Nelson warned, "if we look to the world and follow its formulas for happiness, we will never know joy. The unrighteous may experience any number of emotions and sensations, but they will never experience joy! Joy is a gift for the faithful."[3]

While it is true that we can't look to the great and spacious building for answers about true joy, we as members of the restored Church must clearly understand that all joy comes through the merits of Jesus

Christ. "Just as the Savior offers peace that 'passeth all understanding' (Philippians 4:7), He also offers an intensity, depth, and breadth of joy that defy human logic or mortal comprehension."[4] In order to experience the Savior's joy, we must first learn what it is and then understand what the price is we must pay to obtain it. Otherwise, with preconceived notions of what true joy entails, we may be disappointed in our ability to find it and keep it—especially during our times of trial and adversity.

Over a decade ago, I began pondering the principle of joy and how it relates to the plan of happiness. I thought of the feelings associated with my wedding day and the exciting memories shared with my husband. I then recalled the births of our children and the wonders of looking into their dark eyes and listening to their soft coos and watching their small hands instinctively wrap around my finger. I also considered the delightful and satisfying moments of watching my children's progression, such as when one toddler discovered that playgrounds are for exhilaration or when another learned that large patches of clovers are composed of tiny leaves with delicate patterns. Just remembering such sweet experiences brought me joy all over again!

Looking to the scriptures and the words of the prophets, I continued compiling a list of joyful experiences so I could create my own definition for joy. Each time joy was mentioned in a conference talk or at Church meeting, I made a mental note of it. Over time, I came up with many ideas for joy, including those found in the beauties of nature, the excitement of creating or learning a new skill, the satisfaction of giving our best efforts, the gratitude of repentance and forgiveness, the delight of personal development and divine enlightenment, the sweet love shared with family and friends, the fulfillment of service, and the anticipation of reunion with those we love. What I learned is that all experiences of joy have a spiritual essence to them and that every joy revolves around relationships with others, starting with our most important relationships with Heavenly Father and His Son.

I then discovered the book *Surprised by Joy*, written by the great Christian defender C. S. Lewis. In this autobiography of sorts, Lewis recounts bits of his conversion to Christianity that connect to his pursuit for joy. Before he gained a deep conviction about the Savior, he experienced his first "stabs of joy" through mythology, poetry, and literature. But when he could not compel joy to resurface through these means, his desire to obtain it became an obsession, even a painful haunting because he couldn't have it. He connected the intense moments of joy to the German idea of *sehnsucht*, a deep emotional state of "inconsolable longing" or an insatiable craving. After he embraced the teachings of Jesus Christ and the love of God, he discovered the stabs of joy again and again, and then began sharing his joy with others.[5] The subject of joy became "one of the predominate themes in C. S. Lewis's writings,"[6] and he defined joy as a longing for beauty, a pilgrimage for Home, a yearning for relationships with those we love, and a longing for a relationship with deity. In a collection of letters to a friend, he even concluded, "joy is the serious business of heaven."[7]

Until reading Lewis's conversion story, I hadn't understood several important truths about joy. First of all, because I had taken for granted the many stabs of joy in my life, I didn't realize others would hunger to experience it. I also hadn't considered that joy—unlike pleasure—cannot be forced to materialize and that any and every kind of true joy comes from Heavenly Father's great love for us and because of the gift of His Son. And certainly the last thing I would have guessed is that joy is a "serious" part of God's agenda.

With this new insight, I found myself drawn again and again to King Benjamin's people and their miraculous change of heart. One day while reviewing King Benjamin's remarkable address, the Spirit helped me realize—with overwhelming joy, I might add—that this prophet had outlined the same basic steps of joy I had felt prompted to write down just days before: obedience to God, access to the Savior's Atonement, remembering the Father and the Son, and taking upon the name of Christ through covenant. Truly, "this prophet-king understood the developmental process of serious discipleship"[8] and guided his people though the process of coming unto Christ and becoming His disciples.

From this great prophet, I learned discipleship to the Savior is not only the best prescribed pathway to our personal joy, but it also the means of gaining an enduring relationship with Heavenly Father and endearing relationships with our loved ones.

A thread of King Benjamin's address is included in the following pages. The next four chapters of this book discuss the joys of coming unto the Savior through obedience, sacrifice, remembering, and covenant making. The following three chapters focus on the joys of keeping our covenants to bring others unto Christ. This book is my testimony of the marvelous and priceless gift of the Savior's joy—that which is bestowed upon us by Heavenly Father and through His Holy Spirit. As you read on, I hope you will be excited and inspired to know and experience a greater appreciation for discipleship with the Master and thereby claim His joy in this life and in the eternities hereafter.

Notes

1. Russell M. Nelson, "Joy and Spiritual Survival," *Ensign*, November 2016.
2. Merriam-Webster, s.v. "joy (n.)," accessed August 25, 2017, www.merriam-webster.com/dictionary/joy.
3. Nelson, "Joy and Spiritual Survival."
4. Ibid.
5. C. S. Lewis, *Surprised by Joy: The Shape of My Early Life* (New York: Harcourt, 1966), 7, 16–17, 19, 72–73, 166–69, 238.
6. "Jerry Root: What Was C. S. Lewis's Definition of Joy?" AskQuestions.tv, accessed September 1, 2017, http://askquestions.tv/dr-jerry-root-what-was-c-s-lewiss-definition-of-joy.
7. C. S. Lewis, *Letters to Malcom: Chiefly on Prayer* (New York: Harcourt Brace Jovanovich, 1964), 93.
8. Neal A. Maxwell, "King Benjamin's Manual of Discipleship," *Ensign*, January 1992.

1: Obedience to God—a Foundation of *Joy*

While serving as a missionary in a beautiful village of southern Taiwan, I lived with my companion in a two-story home with an attached one-story kitchen area. One morning, we noticed the blanket we had hung out to dry on the cement wall of the upper roof had fallen down onto the top of the kitchen roof below it. I was about to suggest using the bars on the windows as stairs and climbing from the top roof down to the lower roof. That way, I could attach the blanket to a piece of twine and have my companion lift it back up. Then, I could simply make a loop at the bottom of the string, place my foot in it, and have my companion pull me back up.

But before this idea had left my tongue, I received a very distinct impression from Heavenly Father through the Holy Ghost not to climb down. I mentally argued that I had practically grown up on a farm and was quite capable of such an easy task. Again, the Spirit warned me not to do it. Disregarding these feelings, I stepped down the bars to the kitchen roof below. The blanket went back up just fine, but as I began my ascent upward, the twine snapped in half. I fell eight feet to the kitchen roof below and broke through its fiberglass material! Luckily, my fall was softened by a large bag of ground breakfast cereal on a cabinet inside the kitchen.

As I came to my senses, I looked up through the hole to realize that I had fallen directly between two steel beams. Had I come down an inch to the right or left, I would have hit one of the beams and likely broken some bones, or I would have fallen onto another cement wall surrounding the property of our home. Either way, I knew I had been protected from disaster and was grateful that Heavenly Father provides for His missionaries.

Though I was sure this embarrassing ordeal was over, I didn't anticipate the events that followed. That week, every appointment we had made was cancelled and every door we knocked on was quickly closed. No one would listen to our message, and we didn't make a single contact in five or six consecutive days. Nothing like this had happened during the entire six months I had been serving. Exasperated, I wondered out loud why we weren't having success. At this point, the Spirit whispered to me again. This time it wasn't the urgent voice of warning; it was simply an impression that our proselyting difficulties were the direct results of my disobedience to God. With deep sorrow, I pled for forgiveness and soon our missionary progress resumed.

I have never forgotten the lessons of that week. I learned that my relationship with Heavenly Father comes with great responsibility. Certainly, He respects my agency, but if I expect to be guided "in wisdom's paths" and to be "blessed, prospered, and preserved" (Mosiah 2:36), I need to obey His commands. Ultimately, I discovered that obedience to God is the fundamental price for receiving the Savior's joy, for no one can experience real joy without doing things God's way.

Obedience in All Things

At our baptisms into the Church of Jesus Christ of Latter-day Saints, we covenanted to obey God's commandments and to follow His Son. Obedience—the most important responsibility in our relationship to Heavenly Father—demonstrates our love to Him and His Son as we keep the commandments (see John 14:15). The pathway of joy has always been founded upon the principle of obedience, for "when we obtain any blessing from God, it is by obedience to that law upon which it is predicated" (D&C 130:21). President Gordon B. Hinckley declared, "The happiness of the Latter-day Saints, the peace of the Latter-day Saints, the progress of the Latter-day Saints, the prosperity of the Latter-day Saints, and the eternal salvation and exaltation of this people lie in walking in obedience to the counsels of the priesthood of God."[1]

OBEDIENCE TO GOD

That they might rejoice (see Mosiah 2:4), King Benjamin had taught his people to "keep the commandments of the Lord, *in all things which he hath commanded you*" (Mosiah 2:13; emphasis added).

Obedience in "all things" covers a continuum of choices and several levels of commitment, starting with conformity in keeping certain commandments and followed by hearkening to God's Spirit and aligning our will to His.

Keeping God's commandments. Unlike King Benjamin's people, we are not required to follow the law of Moses. Yet Heavenly Father still expects us to comply with specific laws, including the Ten Commandments, the Word of Wisdom, and the law of chastity. These commandments are pretty clear-cut—you simply keep them or you do not. God will never compel us to obey these commandments, but He wants us to exercise our faith in obedience so we will receive the joys upon which they are predicated: physical health from the Word of Wisdom, financial stability from the law of tithing, and physical and emotional protection from the law of chastity.

President Spencer W. Kimball confirmed the importance of this lowest level of obedience: "Peace, joy, satisfaction, happiness, growth, [and] contentment, all come with the righteous living of the commandments of God."[2] Others have likewise taught that "if we want to experience the inexpressible joy of gospel living and feel of Christ's atoning mercies, obedience to all, and not just a select few, of God's commandments is the only way. . . . When obedience becomes a quest, it is no longer an irritation."[3]

Hearkening to God's Spirit. Even at this most basic level of compliance, we qualify for the sweet companionship of God's Spirit. Once we are willing to keep the "thou shalt" and "thou shalt not" commandments, we then progress to hearkening to His specific promptings through the Spirit. King Benjamin explained that God first requires us to keep His commandments and "secondly, he doth require that ye should do as he hath commanded you" (Mosiah 2:22, 24). Through the Holy Ghost, our Father provides us with specific warnings and directs how and when and where to serve Him and our fellow man. Our obedience at this stage demonstrates that our private religious behaviors are just as important as our public ones.

Aligning our will to God's. Eventually, our obedience to God's commandments and to His Spirit will raise us to a higher level of commitment. Over time and through our continued obedience, we will learn that we "are eternally indebted to [our] heavenly Father" and that we will want to make covenants with Him, align our will to His, and "render to him all that [we] have and are" (Mosiah 2:34). Working toward this obedience is critical to gaining the Savior's joys of mortality and eternal life.

A Relationship of Trust Starts with Knowing the Goodness of God

As God's children, we must trust our Heavenly Parent enough to obey Him at all levels of obedience and thereby experience the joys of a relationship with Him. One mother I know learned more about this type of trust when her young son "ran away" to the backyard after being forced again to practice the piano. After an hour of misery for both of them, the son came back inside crying because he felt unloved. Sensing failure for mishandling yet another power struggle, the mother apologized through her own tears, and the two snuggled together under a blanket for a long talk. Because she sensed her son's disobedience was more about trust than his ability or his desire to please, the mother tried to emphasize the importance of trust and obedience as well as the critical nature of agency and making good choices to be responsible. She promised that she wouldn't ask him to do anything that would hurt him and then pled that he would trust her—even if it meant doing something hard. As peace enveloped them, the Spirit whispered to the mother that the joys of a relationship with her son were inherently tied to her ability to show love and to be trustworthy as a parent. Then, and only then, would her son trust her enough to obey her wishes. And then, and only then, would their relationship deepen and mature.

Because the joys of our relationship with God are also linked to our ability to trust Him, we must clearly know how we can place our confidence in Him. Joseph Smith taught that for us to "exercise faith in God unto life and salvation" we need three things: "the idea that [God] actually exists; a *correct* idea of his character, perfections, and attributes; and an actual knowledge that the course of life which [we are] pursuing is according to the divine will."[4]

Looking at the first two conditions of an effectual faith, we can see that trust in God hinges on knowing that He lives and knowing who He is. Both add meaning, purpose, and joy to mortality, and both provide a clearer vision for our desired destination. The scriptures and the words of the prophets teach us that God does live and that He is the first member of the Godhead; He is the Father of our spirits; and He is omnipresent, all knowing, all-powerful, all creative, and all loving. King Benjamin referred to the perfect character of Heavenly Father as "the goodness of God, and his matchless power, and his wisdom, and his patience, and his long-suffering towards the children of men" (Mosiah 4:6).

As we study the goodness of God, we find that all the joyful gifts of mortality and the joyful promises of eternal life and everything in between are given because of His love. His entire agenda is built upon His love and charity for you and me and all of His children. President Dieter F. Uchtdorf said that God is "filled with an infinite measure of holy, pure, and indescribable love," and "He loves every one of us, even those who are flawed, rejected, awkward, sorrowful, or broken. God's love is so great that He loves even the proud, the selfish, the arrogant, and the wicked."[5] Heavenly Father knows and loves every one of His children individually—regardless of what we do with our agency!

The underlying purpose of all of God's actions, laws, and divine communication is to provide the glorious joys of "immortality and eternal life of man" (Moses 1:39). Heavenly Father loves us so much that He is not only willing to share with us *all He hath* (see D&C 84:38) but also willing to allow us to become *all that He is*. In fact, our Father's greatest joy comes as we progress spiritually and become like Him. Elder Neal A. Maxwell declared that "God is very serious about the joy of His children! Why should we be surprised? God desires us to become more like Him so we can go home to Him. He is a perfect Father!"[6]

Nephi reiterated these truths by comparing the love of God to the tree of life. In his vision, he discovered that this tree and this divine love "sheddeth itself abroad in the hearts of the children of men; wherefore, it is the most desirable above all things . . . *and the most joyous to the soul*" (1 Nephi 11:22–23; emphasis added). The tree of life provides the glorious happiness to those who wish to partake of its fruit. To gain God's love is the reason "men are" upon the earth, and it is the means by which "they might have joy" (2 Nephi 2:25) and have the "Potential to Become like Heavenly Father" (2 Nephi 2:25, footnote *d*). God's love is therefore explicitly offered so that we may experience everlasting joy, become purified as He is pure, and gain immortality and eternal life with Him and our families.

We should rejoice knowing the God over many worlds and the Father of many children knows and loves us individually. With great awe and gratitude, we must discover again and again His specific concern and attention to us and our loved ones. We must be grateful that He can anticipate our needs so completely and then orchestrate time and circumstances and others for our good. And then we must realize that He can do the same for everyone else!

As we understand His love for us personally, we can trust that He will never ask us to do anything that doesn't benefit us in some significant way. His laws of obedience are simply part of His great love for us, just as Joseph Smith declared: "As God has designed our happiness—and the happiness of all His creatures, he never has—He never will institute an ordinance or give a commandment to His people that is not calculated in its nature to promote that happiness which He has designed, and which will not end in the greatest amount of good and glory to those who become the recipients of His law and ordinances."[7] Gaining this joy is why the Lord counsels us to "trust in that Spirit which leadeth to do good—yea, to do justly, to walk humbly, to judge righteously" (D&C 11:12).

Interestingly enough, learning of God's great goodness and His perfect attributes does more than simply improving our trust in Him. It also blesses us to know the characteristics of others. First of all, it helps us understand the workings of the adversary. For example, years ago, after months of a lingering illness, I woke up late and discovered I had missed several children before they had gone to school—again. As I passed my weary reflection in the mirror, the thought came to my mind, *You are ugly*. A bit shocked, I took a moment to think through this notion, and then in an incredulous tone, I replied aloud to the adversary, "Okay, I don't look that great today, and I don't feel that great today. But I am *not* ugly!" I realized then and there that Heavenly Father *has not* and *will never* send me messages that I am inferior, insignificant, or incapable. It is simply not in His character to do so. Whenever positive, encouraging, and uplifting thoughts come into my mind, I know with surety they are from God, and whenever any negative and destructive thoughts come, I know "with a perfect knowledge" they are from Satan (Moroni 7:17).

The more we understand that God is serious about our joy, the more we know that the adversary seeks to interrupt our rejoicings (see Alma 30:22).[8] Satan tries to plant overwhelming feelings of self-doubt, inadequacy, and unwarranted guilt in our minds, and then he tries to convince us that these thoughts come from God Himself! Satan doesn't care about building a relationship with us. All he wants is to ensnare us through addictive behaviors and then use us to perform his evil work. He doesn't care about our happiness, "for he seeketh that all men might be miserable like unto himself" (2 Nephi 2:27), and "the devil will not support his children at the last day, but doth speedily drag them down to hell" (Alma 30:60). The adversary will utilize any number of tricks to distort our perception of our true relationship with God and to change our willingness to trust and obey Him. If we are not watchful unto prayer and obedience, we will allow Satan to erode our spiritual sensitivities. King Benjamin said that if a man will "list to obey the evil spirit" and he "remaineth and dieth in his sins, the same drinketh damnation to his own soul; for he receiveth for his wages an everlasting punishment, having transgressed the law of God contrary to his own knowledge" (Mosiah 2:32–33).

Besides understanding the character of the adversary, the other thing that can happen when we "come to a knowledge of the goodness of God" (Mosiah 4:6) is that we better comprehend ourselves.[9] One friend learned more about herself and her relationship to God while doing some family history work. During most of her hour drive to a family history center, she pled with Heavenly Father that He would verify whether a certain individual was indeed part of her family. When she got there, she was guided to find someone who confirmed her queries, and she left the building not only satisfied but elated her prayers had been answered. Just after she jumped into her car, however, an old man approached her, hoping she could give him some money for lunch that cold day. Perhaps because she was in such a good mood, she obliged his request and started on her way home. Even before she left the parking lot, this phrase came to her mind: "Are we not all beggars? Do we not all depend upon the same Being, even God, for all the substance which we have . . . ?" (Mosiah 4:19). Overwhelmed at this prompting, she realized her entire morning had been spent begging Heavenly Father to provide her with answers. She not only depended upon God for everything of significance in her life, but He had also "poured out His Spirit" and caused her heart to be filled with joy (see Mosiah 4:20) in doing His work.

To stress their everlasting reliance upon God, King Benjamin reminded his people of their essential need to breathe, saying, God "has created you from the beginning, and is preserving you from day to day, by lending you breath, that ye may live and move and do according to your own will, and even supporting you from one moment to another" (Mosiah 2:21). Recognizing our dependence upon God awakens us "to a sense of [our] nothingness, and [our] worthless and fallen state" (Mosiah 4:5). This mortal "nothingness" not only contrasts our insignificance to God's great majesty but it also explains our tendency to waver in our commitment when life gets hard or when temptations come our way. King Benjamin even said we are "less than the dust of the earth" (Mosiah 4:2; see also Mosiah 2:25), a Book of Mormon expression that means that "the dust of the earth moveth hither and thither, to the dividing asunder, at the command of our great and everlasting God" (Helaman 12:8), "whereas men rebel against his will."[10]

Though we are beggars and unreliable in our obedience, our souls are still of great worth in the sight of God (see D&C 18:10). President Uchtdorf explained that when "compared to God, man is nothing; yet we are everything to God."[11] He loves us unconditionally, and He recognizes our shortcomings, but He doesn't hold them against us. It is beyond our understanding that "while against the backdrop of infinite creation we may appear to be nothing, we have a spark of eternal fire burning within our breast. We have the incomprehensible promise of exaltation—worlds without end—within our grasp. And it is God's great desire to help us reach it."[12]

Joyous Assurances from Our Heavenly King

Knowing *about* God and His wondrous love is not the same as *knowing God*. A belief of God's existence and a testimony of His characteristics are critical to our trust in Heavenly Father, yet these two aspects of our faith only provide the beginning of the joys we can receive through our budding relationship with Him. The third condition—the "knowledge that the course of life which [we are] pursuing is according to the divine will"—builds our trust as Heavenly Father communicates His assurances to us and as we come to know that our progress is consistent with His will and that He is pleased with our efforts.

Because we are not in His presence, our relationship with God develops through these spiritual exchanges. We pray to Him and He communicates to us through His Spirit. Heavenly Father's divine messages through the Holy Ghost are heavenly validation—God's way of reassuring us that something is true or valid in our lives. These assurances are a type of divine witness or confirmation that demonstrates His understanding of our feelings and the circumstances of our lives, His acceptance of our service and sacrifices, as well as His approval of our standing or worthiness before Him.[13] Validation from God is a personal and priceless gift, for it powerfully increases our love and devotion and gratitude toward Him, and it deepens our trust and obedience to Him and His Spirit. Over time, Heavenly Father's validation gives us the knowledge that we are on the right path and living according to His will.

Because the Holy Ghost is the medium through which we receive Heavenly Father's assurances and His divinely bestowed blessings, we should often consider the joys of this companionship—or the special relationship we enjoy—with our Father's Spirit.

S stands for "Swell within your breasts." By planting the "seed" of truth in our hearts (see Alma 32:27–28), we can feel the Holy Ghost. Receiving communication from Heavenly Father is a spiritual and a physical experience. Some people describe feeling the Holy Ghost as a "burning in your bosom," but most recognize the Spirit as a peaceful, comforting, or happy feeling inside or a "warm shiver and a tingle which went through my body."[14] God's assurances and communications to us can include peace, faith, direction, warning, comfort, satisfaction, and joy.

E stands for "Enlarge my soul." Through His Spirit and because of His Son, Heavenly Father can magnify our spiritual, mental, and physical abilities. Parley P. Pratt explained it the following way:

> [The Holy Spirit] quickens all the intellectual faculties, increases, enlarges, expands and purifies all the natural passions and affections, and adapts them, by the gift of wisdom, to their lawful use. It inspires, develops, cultivates and matures all the fine toned sympathies, joys, tastes, kindred feelings and affections of our nature. It inspires virtue, kindness, goodness, tenderness, gentleness and charity. It develops beauty of person, form and features. It tends to health, vigor, animation and social feeling. It develops and invigorates all the faculties of the physical and intellectual man. It strengthens, invigorates and gives tone to the nerves. In short, it is, as it were, marrow to the bone, joy to the heart, light to the eyes, music to the ears, and life to the whole being.[15]

E stands for "Enlighten my understanding." To help us learn to trust and obey Him at deeper levels, Heavenly Father also imparts His Holy Spirit to "enlighten [our minds]" and "fill [our souls] with joy" (D&C 11:13). "By the power of the Holy Ghost [we] may know the truth of all things" (Moroni 10:5). With heaven-sent light, the Spirit expands our knowledge, giving us added understanding, insights, and awareness to certain concepts and providing us with revelation, guidance, and wisdom to act in certain situations.

D stands for "Delicious to me." As we "receive the Holy Ghost,"[16] our seed of faith grows and we "know that the gospel is being written in [our hearts], that [our] conversion is happening, as the word of the Lord from His prophets, past and present, feels more and more delicious to [our souls]."[17] In this inviting and sanctifying process—made possible by the Atonement of Jesus Christ and through the Holy Ghost, we are blessed with the *fruits of the Spirit*: "love, joy, peace, longsuffering, gentleness, goodness, faith, meekness, [and] temperance" (Galatians 5:22–23).

To sum up, whenever we receive these divine assurances and blessings through the Spirit, we are drawing nearer to our Heavenly Father and thus experiencing the joy of His Son.

But to improve the quality and quantity of these wonderful assurances from God, we must remember that Heavenly Father respects our choices, and it is *our actions* that determine the depth and magnitude of our relationships with Him. President Uchtdorf taught the following:

> We improve our relationship with our Heavenly Father by learning of Him, communing with Him, by repenting of our sins, and by actively following Jesus Christ, for "no man cometh unto the Father, but by [Christ]." To strengthen our relationship with God, we need some meaningful time alone with Him. Quietly focusing on daily personal prayer and scripture study, always aiming to be worthy of a current temple recommend—these will be some wise investments of our time and efforts to draw closer to our Heavenly Father.[18]

It is nearly incomprehensible that we are children of such a magnificent and everlasting Being and that we can have a personal and spiritual relationship with Him!

In His great plan of happiness, we rejoice in our ability to communicate with Heavenly Father in prayer and to demonstrate our love through obedience. We rejoice knowing that the more we will receive His line-upon-line assurances through the whisperings of His Spirit, the more we will trust in His promises, and eventually receive the joys of returning to His presence. And at that day, "nothing is going to startle us more when we pass through the veil to the other side than to realize how well we know our Father and how familiar his face is to us."[19] How eternally grateful we must be for the joys of this relationship! And "O how [we] ought to thank [our] heavenly King!" (Mosiah 2:19).

Because our level of continued obedience will always parallel our overall level of joy, King Benjamin's counsel is just as relevant to us today: "Believe in God; believe that he is, and that he created all things, both in heaven and in earth; believe that he has all wisdom, and all power, both in heaven and in earth; believe that man doth not comprehend all the things which the Lord can comprehend" (Mosiah 4:9). Furthermore, "Do as ye have hitherto done" (Mosiah 2:31) in keeping the commandments, for this is all that God requires of us (see Mosiah 2:22).

I testify that our responsibility to obey God will not only become our greatest defense against snares of the adversary but it will also bless us with the Savior's joys, including the peace and happiness of the Spirit and a strengthened relationship with our Eternal Father. As we strive to be obedient in all things, we will thereby be "blessed in all things, both temporal and spiritual; and if [we] hold out faithful to the end [we will be] received into heaven, that thereby [we] may dwell with God in a state of never-ending happiness" (Mosiah 2:41). May we all strive to obtain the priceless joys of a relationship with our Heavenly Father!

Notes

1. Gordon B. Hinckley, "'If Ye Be Willing and Obedient,'" *Ensign*, December 1971.
2. Spencer W. Kimball, in *Conference Report*, April 1952.
3. Mary Ellen Smoot, "We Are Instruments in the Hands of God," *Ensign*, November 2000.
4. As quoted in N. B. Lundwall, comp., *A Compilation Containing the Lectures on Faith* (Salt Lake City: Bookcraft, n.d.), 33; emphasis in original.
5. Dieter F. Uchtdorf, "The Love of God," *Ensign*, November 2009.
6. Neal A. Maxwell, "Becoming a Disciple," *Ensign*, June 1996.
7. Joseph Smith, in B. H. Roberts, *History of the Church* (Salt Lake City: Deseret Book, 1980), 5:135.
8. President Russell M. Nelson also declared that "anything that opposes Christ or His doctrine will interrupt our joy. That includes the philosophies of men, so abundant online and in the blogosphere." ("Joy and Spiritual Survival," *Ensign*, November 2016.)
9. The Prophet Joseph Smith said, "If men do not comprehend the character of God, they do not comprehend themselves" (*History of the Church*, 6:303.)
10. Bruce R. McConkie, *Mormon Doctrine*, 2nd ed. (Salt Lake City: Bookcraft, 1979), 210.
11. Dieter F. Uchtdorf, "You Matter to Him," *Ensign*, November 2011.
12. Ibid.
13. Richard G. Scott tells us that God "will confirm the correctness of our choices His way. That confirmation generally comes through packets of help found along the way. We discover them by being spiritually sensitive. They are like notes from a loving Father as evidence of His approval. If, in trust, we begin something which is not right, He will let us know before we have gone too far. We sense that help by recognizing

troubled or uneasy feelings." ("Learning to Recognize Answers to Prayer," *Ensign,* November 1989.)

14. Janet Thomas, "Feeling the Spirit," *New Era*, September 2010; see also Merrilee Browne Boyack, "Helping Children Recognize the Holy Ghost," *Ensign*, December 2013.
15. Parley P. Pratt, *Key to the Science of Theology*, 5th ed. (Salt Lake City: George Q. Cannon & Sons, 1891), 101–102; see also Tad R. Callister, *The Infinite Atonement* (Salt Lake City: Deseret Book, 2000), 268.
16. Henry B. Eyring, "The Holy Ghost as Your Companion," *Ensign,* November 2015; see also *Handbook 2: Administering the Church* (2010), 20.3.10.
17. D. Todd Christofferson, "When Thou Art Converted," *Ensign*, May 2004.
18. Dieter F. Uchtdorf, "Of Things That Matter Most," *Ensign*, November 2010.
19. Ezra Taft Benson, "Jesus Christ—Gifts and Expectations" (Brigham Young University devotional, December 10, 1974), 8, speeches.byu .edu.

2: Our Joy Shall Be in the Lord

Elder David A. Bednar taught that the tree of life—or the love of God—is also "a symbol for the life, ministry, and sacrifice of the Savior" and that its pure and white fruit symbolizes the sweet "blessings of the Atonement."[1] As noted, we receive God's love through the joys of obedience, and we thereby experience further joy though a deepening relationship with Heavenly Father. But to fully understand these messages of theology, we now will look at what Elder Neal A. Maxwell termed "correct Christology,"[2] for seeking and finding our ultimate happiness, satisfaction, and joy can only come through a relationship with Jesus Christ and by virtue of His atoning sacrifice.

Elder Jeffrey R. Holland taught that "it's important for every individual to have a relationship with Christ because salvation is a personal, individual experience."[3]

In striving for this joyous blessing, we must first realize that because the unity and purpose of the Savior and His Father are the same, "the words or deeds of either of them would be the words and deeds of the other in the same circumstance;" in fact, most scriptures "do not even bother to distinguish the Father from the Son, simply because it doesn't make any difference which God is involved."[4] As we receive revelation through the Spirit, we accordingly can consider the divine words and impressions as from both Heavenly Father and Jesus Christ. And because

They are "at one" with each other, we know that the Savior's joys are also the Father's joys.

Although they are one with each other, our relationship with Jesus Christ is different from our relationship with Heavenly Father. "Our relationship with the Father is supreme, paramount, and preeminent over all others."[5] We "love and serve both the Father and the Son," but we follow the Savior's example to worship and pray to the Father.[6] On the other hand, our formal relationship with Christ began at baptism. This is a "personal master/apprentice relationship with the Master himself."[7] It is our faith and repentance that "qualify us to enter [this] relationship, just as the Savior's Atonement qualifies him to enter it."[8] Over time and through our experiences in this discipleship, we deepen our appreciation of His love and sacrifice and then we are motivated to sacrifice for His cause and claim His "glad tidings of great joy" (Mosiah 3:3).

The Savior's Joys of Discipleship Come through Sacrifice

Several years ago, our daughter came home from an inspirational meeting on the Savior's Atonement. After she shared several meaningful stories, her father and I were shocked when she asked why we didn't talk more about the Atonement in our home. Our initial reaction was, "Isn't that what we've been doing all along?!" Then for days we marveled that hours of scripture study and family discussions about Jesus Christ hadn't translated into a correct understanding of His sacrifice and how to claim the joys offered by Him.

As we were trying to redirect our gospel discussions at home, my husband was called to serve as bishop of our ward. He then felt added weight to help members embrace the blessings of Christ's Atonement. With our experiences at home, he knew how easy it was to disconnect our daily struggles with our dependence on the Lord. At a leadership training meeting, he earnestly asked, "What can we do to help others feel the need and ask for the Savior's divine help in their lives?" The first response was counsel to help others learn all they can about God's Only Begotten Son. But then Elder M. Russell Ballard rose to add a sobering response, "You must take them to Gethsemane. You must take them to Golgotha." Elder Ballard wasn't talking about visiting these sacred places to change and repent and grow, but he meant that "the best way—the only way— to persuade people to repent and come unto Christ is to get them—to get us—to think about what He has done for us and especially about what He has suffered for us."[9]

King Benjamin taught that Jesus suffered "temptations, and pain of body, hunger, thirst, and fatigue, even more than man can suffer, except it be unto death; for behold, blood cometh from every pore, so great shall be his anguish for the wickedness and the abominations of his people" (Mosiah 3:7). "His suffering was beyond our imagination. His grief was beyond our comprehension. His pain was beyond utterance. His struggle was beyond endurance."[10] Yet, "it was not physical pain, nor mental anguish alone, that caused Him to suffer such torture as to produce an extrusion of blood from every pore; but a spiritual agony of soul such as only God was capable of experiencing."[11] Christ's agony continued after Gethsemane with the betrayal of Judas, the illegal arrest, the abandonment of His apostles, the denial of Peter, the false accusations in the presence of Pilate, the scourging of leather strips, the crown of thorns, the solitary walk to Golgotha, the painful execution on the cross, and the feeling of being forsaken by His Father.

Perhaps we might claim that as Son of God, His "superhuman powers"[12] protected Him from suffering. But He was intentionally born in the flesh that He might experience mortality in the fullest sense. Thus, He didn't intellectualize our mortal plight of physical, spiritual, and emotional pain. He voluntarily "let his humanity take precedence over his divinity" and He "both felt and tasted the whole of it." Moreover, "that he also had godly powers did not make his suffering any less excruciating, any less poignant, or any less real. To the contrary, it is for this very reason that his suffering was more, not less, than his mortal counterparts could experience."[13]

But, we may ask, why would anyone *willingly* suffer in this manner? President Russell M. Nelson verified that "Jesus suffered deeply because He loves us deeply."[14] The Savior knows and loves us intimately. He knew that through the Fall of Adam and because of our own transgressions, we would be spiritually and physically separated from the Father, a condition that would frustrate our relationship with God. Because of these challenges, the Father's plan of salvation—or simply the gospel of Jesus Christ—is carried out by the Savior.[15] The purpose of His great "At-one-ment" is to bring us back, physically and spiritually, to our Heavenly Father. The Savior's sacrifice is offered to each of us, one by one, that we can become "children of Christ" (Mosiah 5:7) by obeying the commandments from His Father and thereby becoming reconciled to God. Therefore when we *come unto Christ*, He brings us unto His Father.

Jesus Christ, "He who bore the atoning yoke has asked us to 'take my yoke upon you, and learn of me' (Matt. 11:29)."[16] This is simply an invitation to become His disciples and to "humbly do his will and allow him to guide and direct our lives."[17] Just as a wooden yoke makes it possible to balance a heavy burden between two oxen and to yield the greatest pulling power as a team, we are yoked to the Savior and He becomes our partner in "[working] out [our] salvation" (Philippians 2:12) and strengthening our relationship to Heavenly Father. Because His "yoke is easy, [and His] burden is light" (Matthew 11:30), the Master can teach us—His apprentices—how to experience His joys and to thereby "find rest unto [our] souls" (Matthew 11:29).

As we take upon the yoke of discipleship to Jesus Christ, we quickly learn that our own sacrifice must be added to His great atoning sacrifice. We remember that sacrifice in the law of Moses required Christ's disciples to offer the firstlings of their flocks and the first fruits of their fields. But after His last and infinite sacrifice, He proclaimed, "Your sacrifices and your burnt offerings shall be done away . . . . And ye shall offer for a sacrifice unto me a broken heart and a contrite spirit" (3 Nephi 9:19–20). It is "unto all those who have a broken heart and a contrite spirit" that Christ "offereth himself a sacrifice for sin, to answer the ends of the law" (2 Nephi 2:7).

Offering a broken heart and a contrite spirit means we are *willing to believe* and *willing to act*. This joint commitment of belief and action means we are "humble, contrite, repentant, and meek—that is, receptive to the will of God."[18] Nephi exhibited a broken heart and a contrite spirit when he cried to "know of the mysteries of God" (1 Nephi 2:16) and when he vowed to "go and do the things which the Lord [had] commanded [him]" (1 Nephi 3:7). Offering a broken heart and a contrite spirit is thus another way of saying we have faith to do something. President Dieter F. Uchtdorf explained that "faith is a strong conviction about something we believe—a conviction so strong that it moves us to do things that we otherwise might not do."[19]

Offering a broken heart and a contrite spirit demonstrates a deeper level of sacrifice to God. Just as we comply with basic commandments of God, we likewise sacrifice on a basic level when we offer our tithes and fast offerings to the Lord. And just as hearkening to God's Spirit is evidence of greater obedience to Him, sacrificing our broken heart and contrite spirit shows a more serious commitment in our discipleship to Christ. This deepened sacrifice is dovetailed with our deepened obedience to God, for our willingness to believe and willingness to do make it so much easier to hearken to the whisperings of His Spirit. We thus strive to obey with exactness, we pray in earnestness, we repent completely, and we serve faithfully. And eventually we hope to fully sacrifice in our discipleship to the Savior as we "offer [our] whole souls" unto Him and His Father (Omni 1:26).

SACRIFICE TO GOD

Repentance Leads to the Joys of the Atonement's Cleansing Power

Repentance is the first part of our sacrifice as a disciple of Christ. To illustrate the effects of sin, we can picture dipping our hands into black tar. Even if only the tips of our fingers touch the sticky substance, we are still unclean and separated from God, "for no unclean thing can . . . dwell in his presence" (Moses 6:57). But what if the black tar could never be removed? In other words, what if our mistakes and sins caused long-term consequences for ourselves and others that could never be resolved? What if we could never receive forgiveness from others or from God? How could our lives progress if this disappointment and sorrow and guilt never left? Truly, if the Savior had not atoned for our sins, we would *always* feel regret and hopelessness in our ability to change for the better.

Since justice demands a penalty to be paid for sins, God provides mercy through the sacrifice of His Only Begotten Son. The Savior's Atonement works like a bar of soap, which not only cleans our hands from the effects of sin, but also takes away any sorrow resulting from poor choices and gives everlasting hope that things will get better and that we can change. Repentance means reaching for the soap and doing our part to scrub away as much of the tar as possible, knowing that our efforts merely qualify us for the Savior's redemption. Hence, the hopeful and joyous news of the gospel of Christ is that except for the sin of denying the Holy Ghost (Alma 39:5–6), you and I and our loved ones *can* repent and become as clean as on the day of our baptisms!

The key to obtaining and enjoying the blessings of repentance is first believing in Christ's cleansing power and then doing whatever is necessary to receive the joys of redemption: feel godly sorrow, confess and forsake our sins, forgive others, and rectify problems caused by our deeds. King Benjamin thus exhorted the Nephites to "believe in God" and to "believe that ye must repent of your sins and forsake them, and humble yourselves before God; and ask in sincerity of heart that he would forgive you." Then he emphasized: "And now, if you believe all these things see that ye do them" (Mosiah 4:9–10).[20]

The joyful rewards of clean hands are scattered throughout time and throughout scripture. King Benjamin testified that they who exercise faith in the Lord Jesus Christ and repent of their transgressions will receive "a remission of their sins" and "peace of conscience" (Mosiah 4:3). True repentance leads to divine forgiveness—which helps us "rejoice with exceedingly great joy" (Mosiah 3:13). Alma the Younger explained this joy when he said, "I could remember my pains no more . . . . And oh, what joy, and what marvelous light I did behold; yea, my soul was filled with joy as exceeding as was my pain!" (Alma 36:19–20). Thus, "joy is much deeper than simply passing moments of contentment or feelings of happiness. Real joy, or 'everlasting joy' (2 Nephi 8:11), comes from experiencing the power of the Atonement through sincere repentance and from a spiritual confirmation that we can be redeemed from sin through the Lord Jesus Christ and inherit eternal life."[21]

Offering Our Best Efforts to Rejoice in the Savior's Grace

In our desire for eternal life, however, we may be surprised to learn that simply receiving a "remission of sin is not the only or even the ultimate purpose of the gospel."[22] That is because returning to God involves not only "turning away from some things, such as dishonesty, pride, anger, and impure thoughts" but it also implies "turning toward other things, such as kindness, unselfishness, patience, and spirituality."[23] Thankfully and joyfully, the Savior can clean our hands *and* He can purify our hearts through His atoning sacrifice.

King Benjamin aptly taught his people to "[yield] to the enticings of the Holy Spirit, and putteth off the natural man and becometh a saint through the atonement of Christ the Lord" (Mosiah 3:19). We also need the Savior's redeeming power to clean our hands as we try to "put off the natural man," and we require His strengthening power to purify our hearts to "become a saint."

Recognizing their need for both clean hands and a pure heart, King Benjamin's people "viewed themselves in their own carnal state, even less than the dust of the earth" (Mosiah 4:2). In deep humility, they fell to the earth, for "the Spirit carried [his words] into their hearts with such impact that they suddenly saw themselves as they really were—good people, honest people, but people still in a state of unredeemed sin."[24] In willingness to believe in God's plan and to act in faith, they cried out together, "O have mercy, and apply the atoning blood of Christ that we may *receive forgiveness of our sins*, and *our hearts may be purified*; for we believe in Jesus Christ, the Son of God" (Mosiah 4:2; emphasis added). In response to their faith, God "poured out his Spirit upon [them], and . . . caused that [their] hearts should be filled with joy, and . . . caused that [their] mouths should be stopped that [they] could not find utterance, so exceedingly great was [their] joy" (Mosiah 4:20). This joy resulted not only from remission of their sins and peace of conscience, but also from the great hope of their continued sanctification—precisely "the glad tidings of great joy" that had been promised (Mosiah 3:3).

The process of cleaning hands and purifying hearts comes through *God's grace* or *the Savior's grace*. Grace is simply another way of defining Christ's power, made possible by His atoning sacrifice and given through the Spirit. The Bible Dictionary further clarifies that grace is the "divine means of help or strength, given through the bounteous mercy and love of Jesus Christ."[25] Through His grace, all will be raised to immortality and individuals can repent of their sins and "receive strength and assistance to do good works that they otherwise would not be able to maintain if left to their own means."[26] Thus, grace is the power that strengthens us to repent and to forgive, and it is the power that unlocks the gifts of the Spirit that enhance our natural creativity, stamina, abilities, and love for others.

Offering a broken heart and a contrite spirit to obtain these joyful blessings is a belief in His power to strengthen us and the offering of our faithful works. The Savior's grace "allows men and women to lay hold on eternal life and exaltation after they have expended their own best efforts."[27] Our works include anything we do to sacrifice to bless our fellow beings—missionary service, acts of kindness in our homes, or simply forgiving and forgetting others' trespasses against us. Our sacrifices are yoked to the Savior's ultimate sacrifice, and, just as He does with our tithes and offerings, Jesus Christ will generate more of our individual time and efforts than we can create on our own.

We can recall many stories of devoted men and women receiving the Savior's grace. Missionaries offer their service and receive extra energy to work, leaders offer their talents and receive extra insights to bless those they teach, and parents offer their time and energy and receive extra patience for their children. Our daughter experienced this divine strength during a busy semester of high school. She had prayed and fasted for months to know how to arrange her class schedule and was given revelation to add and drop two classes, making it possible to participate in a special needs seminary class. Thrilled with this opportunity, she discovered for herself that Heavenly Father and His Son knew the desires of her heart and were *in the details* of her life. Weeks later, however, she nevertheless became overwhelmed by the demands of schoolwork and extracurricular activities. Sensing I ought to talk to her one night, I found her sitting on her bed. But before thinking about what I should say, I boldly testified that because Heavenly Father had inspired her rearrange her schedule, He would send His Son to sustain her during the school year. As soon as the words left my lips, I knew they were true. But more importantly, *she* knew they were true. What wonder and joy I felt to be strengthened to say just what she needed to hear, and what joy and comfort she felt as the Spirit validated the truth! Because she recognized the Savior's previous help, she had confidence in His future support.

Through His Son, Heavenly Father can definitely purify our hearts, but only through a lifetime of work on our part. "Divine grace is needed by every soul in consequence of the Fall of Adam and also because of man's weaknesses and shortcomings. However, grace cannot suffice without total effort on the part of the recipient. Hence the explanation, 'It is by grace that we are saved, after all we can do' (2 Nephi 25:23)."[28] Thankfully, this means that "we may receive [Christ's] grace before, during, and after the time when we expend our own efforts."[29]

Compared to what the Master does for us, our works as disciples may be quite small, but they will be hard work nonetheless. I love knowing that "I can do all things through Christ which strengtheneth me" (Philippians 4:13), and I testify that we are all capable of extraordinary things—even impossible things—with the strengthening power of His Atonement!

Hope and Healing through the Joy of Christ

Because we actually need *hard things* for our development and refinement, Heavenly Father will bestow upon us all the necessary opportunities and experiences that may help us become yoked to His Son. Elder Maxwell taught that "most of our suffering comes from sin," but "the highest source of suffering appears to be reserved for the innocent who undergo divine tutorial training."[30] Divine tutorials are any tailored, soul-stretching experiences in mortality, such as problems relating to health, grief from the loss of a loved one, distress within the home, demands of varied responsibilities and callings, and simply adversity that comes with life itself.

Close friends have taught us much about divine tutorials through their experience of losing their beautiful daughter. Before her birth, doctors diagnosed Annalee with a rare form of skeletal dysplasia. Annalee came into a world of newborn intensive care treatments, as well as physicians' concerns that extra medical care might be life threatening. We prayed that Annalee's family would have adequate time to get to know her before she returned to her heavenly home, and miraculously, their home was filled with her light for another five months. At her funeral, her father spoke with great passion regarding the gift and power of the Savior's sacrifice, saying that Annalee represented the best the Atonement has to offer. Annalee's mother also noted the pure joy she had experienced while caring for her daughter and while discovering specific ways to be grateful to God. Her conclusion of divine tutorials was, "We get to keep what we become."

Over time, these dear friends learned that just as transgressions can be forgiven and weaknesses can be strengthened through Christ, so can the sorrows of affliction be healed through His divine healing power. The joys of the Savior's hope and healing are found only by offering a broken heart and contrite spirit, a sacrifice of childlike trust and submission of our will to God's will. King Benjamin counseled his people to "[become] as a child, submissive, meek, humble, patient, full of love, willing to submit to all things which the Lord seeth fit to inflict upon him, even as a child doth submit to his father" (Mosiah 3:19). During our challenging times—and though the adversary will tempt us otherwise—we must continue to trust in and obey God and continue to believe and to do, even when we don't understand why.

But how can we meekly endure through the heat of such adversity? President Nelson explained that in order for our Savior "to endure the most excruciating experience ever endured on earth, [He] focused on *joy*."[31] The "joy that was set before him" (Hebrews 12:2) surely "included the joy of cleansing, healing, and strengthening us; the joy of paying for the sins of all who would repent; the joy of making it possible for you and me to return home—clean and worthy—to live with our Heavenly Parents and families."[32]

The way we can likewise endure our own divine tutorials is by focusing on the joys set before us. These joys include the multitude of the Savior's tender mercies that always accompany our trials. Tender mercies are any spiritual manifestation of the Savior's cleansing, strengthening, and healing power. Elder Bednar defined tender mercies as "very personal and individualized blessings, strength, protection, assurances, guidance, loving-kindnesses, consolation, support, and spiritual gifts which we receive from and because of and through the Lord Jesus Christ." Furthermore, "tender mercies do not occur randomly or merely by coincidence. Faithfulness and obedience enable us to receive these important gifts and, frequently, the Lord's timing helps us to recognize them."[33] Examples of tender mercies include the following:

- "the gift of faith"
- "an appropriate sense of personal confidence that reaches beyond our own capacity"
- "repentance and forgiveness of sins"

- "peace of conscience"
- "the persistence and the fortitude that enable us to press forward with cheerfulness through physical limitations and spiritual difficulties"[34]

Because of the sacrifice of the Savior and our willingness to become submissive, meek, and humble, we can expect that "grace shall be as your day"[35] and "as thy days may demand, so thy succor shall be."[36] On the days our needs are more demanding and our hearts heavier, we will be filled with more validation, peace, and guidance. Those will be the times when others step forward and answer our prayers, when scriptural understanding comes quickly or perhaps more clearly than before, and when our intense searching not only satisfies our inquiries but also gives us specific direction to take further steps into a seemingly dark future. We will come to know God as a compassionate and merciful Being who not only understands our overwhelming sorrow but also sends reassurances from His Spirit and grace from His Son to comfort, bless, and sustain us. In fact, President Henry B. Eyring declared, "If you have felt the influence of the Holy Ghost today, you may take it as evidence that the [Savior's] Atonement is working in your life."[37]

Our family has grown to love the paintings of Carl H. Bloch—especially one called, *Consolator*.[38] Representative of mankind partaking of the Savior's atoning sacrifice, the painting depicts Jesus Christ and His outstretched hands bidding welcome to the figures surrounding Him. These include the shackled sinner, the elderly and infirm, the tearful widow and her fatherless children mourning their loss, the skeptic who questions the power of the Christ, and the disciple who clutches his Master's robes in profound reliance.

At one time or another, we will become each of the characters surrounding the Savior, and in all the seasons of our lives, we can know that the pure and delicious fruit of Christ's Atonement is available to us. When we transgress the laws of God, we will become the bound sinner, relying on the Savior's redeeming power. When we are physically weak and spiritually exhausted, we will offer our best efforts to gain His strengthening and enabling power. When we mourn for deep losses, we will rely on the healing power of His grace. When we question His truths, we will ask His Father to send a divine witness of His reality and a reassurance of our divine worth. And, hopefully, through our many experiences, we all will become the seasoned disciple who pays the price to receive the Savior's joys.

With the fruit of the Master's sufferings, I have been cleansed and strengthened and I have been healed of heavy sorrow. Jesus Christ has taken my "infirmities, that his bowels may be filled with mercy, according to the flesh, that he may know according to the flesh how to succor [me] according to [my] infirmities" (Alma 7:12). I know that "there shall be no other name given nor any other way nor means whereby salvation can come unto the children of men, only in and through the name of Christ, the Lord Omnipotent" (Mosiah 3:17). Indeed, no other individual, institution, worldly power, or ennobling concept can redeem me of sin, strengthen me in challenges, and restore my hope, peace, and joy—let alone produce the power to change my nature and to guarantee the promises of salvation and exaltation!

Oh, how we need the joys of the Savior! Just as we need to *know* our Heavenly Father, "a true faith in Christ is more than just knowing about Him or even believing He is divine. It is knowing that His Atonement is real, that its purpose is to transform us, and that it will be available to us as long as that perfecting process takes."[39] Because our Father knew that we would need divine help to return Home, He sent His Only Begotten Son to suffer for our sins, transgressions, and afflictions. Only through Christ can we live and "learn from [our] experience without being condemned by it,"[40] making it possible for us to "progress toward perfection and ultimately realize [our] divine destiny as heirs of eternal life."[41] The problem then is not whether it is possible to become like the Master; it is whether we can stay yoked with Him, offering our broken hearts and contrite spirits to activate the power of His atoning sacrifice in our behalf.[42]

Because "[our] joy shall be in the Lord" (2 Nephi 27:30), we must add our sacrifice to His. In so doing we can claim Jesus Christ as our Savior—the one who saves us—and our Redeemer—the One who has bought us and can cleanse and purify us. Then we will see that His sacrifice makes salvation possible, that He is the reason the plan is perfectly orchestrated, and that He is the reason we find joy in anything![43] He is the "light, the life, and the hope of the world. His way is the path that leads to happiness in this life and eternal life in the world to come. God be thanked for the matchless gift of His divine Son."[44]

Notes

1. David A. Bednar, "Lehi's Dream: Holding Fast to the Iron Rod," *Ensign*, October 2011.
2. Neal A. Maxwell, "The Children of Christ," in Monte S. Nyman and Charles D. Tate Jr., eds., *The Book of Mormon: Mosiah, Salvation Only through Christ* (Provo, UT: Religious Studies Center, 1991), 6.
3. Jeffrey R. Holland, "The Savior Understands Me," LDS.org, accessed September 5, 2017, www.lds.org/media-library/video/2016-03-0021-the-savior-understands-me.
4. Bruce R. McConkie, "Our Relationship with the Lord" (Brigham Young University devotional, March 2, 1982), 6, speeches.byu.edu. Neal A. Maxwell also declared, "Since he and the Father are one in attributes and in purpose, Jesus acts for the Father through divine investiture, sometimes speaking as the Father (D&C 93:3–5)." ("The Children of Christ," in Nyman and Tate, eds., *The Book of Mormon: Mosiah, Salvation Only through Christ*, 6.)
5. McConkie, "Our Relationship with the Lord," 7.
6. Ibid., 3.
7. Bruce C. Hafen and Marie K. Hafen, *The Belonging Heart: The Atonement and Relationships with God and Family* (Salt Lake City: Deseret Book, 1994), 145.
8. Ibid., 152.
9. Thomas B. Griffith, "The Very Root of Christian Doctrine" (Brigham Young University devotional, March 16, 2006), 7, speeches.byu.edu.
10. Yoshihiko Kikuchi, "Do We Know How Much He Went Through?" *New Era*, December 2009.
11. James E. Talmage, *Jesus the Christ: A Study of the Messiah and His Mission According to Holy Scriptures Both Ancient and Modern*, 42nd ed. (Salt Lake City: Deseret Book, 1976), 613.
12. Tad R. Callister, *The Infinite Atonement* (Salt Lake City: Deseret Book, 2000), 117.
13. Ibid., 118–19.
14. Russell M. Nelson, "Jesus Christ—The Master Healer," *Ensign*, November 2005.

15. Bruce R. McConkie has written, "The plan of salvation, for men in this life, is the gospel of Jesus Christ. It comprises all of the laws, ordinances, and performances by conformity to which mortal man is empowered to gain eternal life in the kingdom of God." (*Mormon Doctrine*, 2nd ed. [Salt Lake City: Bookcraft, 1979], 576.) Furthermore, when the resurrected Savior first visited the Nephites, He often explained that He was fulfilling the Father's commandments (for example, see 3 Nephi 16:3, 10, 16; 17:2). Christ also told the people that they would be blessed "if ye shall keep my commandments, which the Father hath commanded me that I should give unto you" (3 Nephi 18:14).
16. Neal A. Maxwell, "Becoming a Disciple," *Ensign*, June 1996.
17. "Lesson 10: Take My Yoke upon You, and Learn of Me," in *New Testament Gospel Doctrine Teacher's Manual* (2002), 40–43.
18. Guide to the Scriptures, "Broken Heart," scriptures.lds.org.
19. Dieter F. Uchtdorf, "Fourth Floor, Last Door," *Ensign*, November 2016.
20. President Thomas S. Monson also explained our need to believe and to do: "Essential to the plan is our Savior, Jesus Christ. Without His atoning sacrifice, all would be lost. It is not enough, however, merely to believe in Him and His mission. We need to work and learn, search and pray, repent and improve. We need to know God's laws and live them. We need to receive His saving ordinances. Only by so doing will we obtain true, eternal happiness." ("The Perfect Path to Happiness," *Ensign*, November 2016.)
21. Craig C. Christensen, "Lessons from the New Testament: The Joy of Repentance," *Ensign*, April 2007.
22. David A. Bednar, "Clean Hands and a Pure Heart," *Ensign*, November 2007.
23. Neil L. Andersen, "'Repent . . . That I May Heal You,'" *Ensign*, November 2009.
24. "Becoming Sons and Daughters of Christ," in *Book of Mormon Student Manual*, 2nd ed. (Church Educational System manual, 1981), 163.
25. Bible Dictionary, "Grace."
26. Ibid.
27. Ibid.
28. Ibid.

29. Bruce C. Hafen, *The Broken Heart: Applying the Atonement to Life's Experiences* (Salt Lake City: Deseret Book, 1989), 156.
30. Neal A. Maxwell, "Thanks Be to God," *Ensign*, July 1982.
31. Russell M. Nelson, "Joy and Spiritual Survival," *Ensign*, November 2016.
32. Ibid. Brad Wilcox further taught: "Jesus doesn't need followers to give Him self-esteem, authority, or power. He stands supreme completely independent of followers. However, He does receive from disciples something that all the esteem, authority, and power in the universe cannot offer: joy." (*The Continuous Atonement* [Salt Lake City: Deseret Book, 2009], 39–40.)
33. David A. Bednar, "The Tender Mercies of the Lord," *Ensign*, May 2005.
34. Ibid.
35. "Come, Come, Ye Saints," *Hymns*, no. 30.
36. "How Firm a Foundation," *Hymns*, no. 85.
37. Henry B. Eyring, "Gifts of the Spirit for Hard Times," *Ensign*, June 2007.
38. Carl H. Bloch, *Consolator*, in Ron Gibbs, *Harmony of the Gospels with the Artwork of Carl Bloch* (Springville, UT: Cedar Fort, Inc., 2014), 168.
39. Wilcox, *The Continuous Atonement*, 3.
40. Bruce C. Hafen, "The Temple and the Natural Order of Marriage," *Ensign*, September 2015; see also John 3:16.
41. "The Family: A Proclamation to the World," *Ensign*, November 2010.
42. Bruce C. Hafen and Marie K. Hafen discuss how our sacrifice initiates the blessings of the Savior's sacrifice. (See *The Contrite Spirit: How the Temple Helps Us Apply Christ's Atonement* [Salt Lake City: Deseret Book, 2015], 38, 42–43.)
43. President Russell M. Nelson likewise testified, "Joy comes from and because of Him. He is the source of all joy." ("Joy and Spiritual Survival.")
44. "The Living Christ: The Testimony of the Apostles," *Ensign*, April 2000.

3: Always Remember to Always *Rejoice*

One of our greatest reasons for rejoicing is that we were created to experience beautiful and joyful relationships with other human beings, especially our family members. As noted, we can enjoy relationships with Heavenly Father and Jesus Christ through our responsibilities of obedience and sacrifice, but as we seek to retain the Savior's joy we can likewise enjoy rich relationships with those around us. "Relationships are the core of our existence because they are the core of God's."[1] He "organizes us into families so that we can grow up in happiness and safety, and so that we can learn to love others selflessly—the key to true joy."[2]

Family associations and friendships are critical to our eternal progression because relationships "provide the friction that wears down our rough edges and sanctifies us. And then, and only then, those relationships become the environment in which those perfected virtues are best enjoyed. We need those virtues not just here, but eternally" with our families in the hereafter.[3] "The divine plan of happiness enables family relationships to be perpetuated beyond the grave,"[4] so we must work on them now if we want them to continue in the next life!

Perhaps because he sees the potential joys of our relationships with loved ones, the adversary strives to destroy our marriages and families. He "has known the plan of salvation from before the Creation. He knows that only in eternal life can those sacred, joyful associations of families endure. Satan would tear us from loved ones and make us miserable. And it is he who plants the seeds of discord in human hearts in the hope that we might be divided and separate."[5] If he can entice us to forget our relationships with and our responsibilities to Heavenly Father and Jesus Christ, we "withdraw [ourselves] from the Spirit of the Lord" (Mosiah 2:36) and are left unprotected without the Holy Ghost. Truly, he who "inviteth and enticeth to sin" (Moroni 7:12) wants us to forget Them so our unchecked thoughts will lead to unbridled tongues and our unkind words will lead to unrestrained behaviors. King Benjamin thus warned: "If ye do not watch yourselves, and your thoughts, and your words, and your deeds, . . . even unto the end of your lives, ye must perish. And now, O man, remember, and perish not" (Mosiah 4:30).

When our oldest child became an adolescent, she and I endured one power struggle after another and contention filled our home on a consistent basis. Both of us offended and both took offense. After praying for guidance and then enrolling in a parenting class with my husband, I was inspired to know that my relationship with my daughter was my prime concern—as opposed to my need to be right or "in control." After that, my husband and I discussed together and with our children the importance of relationships. Recognizing Satan's attack on family relationships helped us understand that fueling the fires of contention was subtly robbing us of the Savior's joy. Gaining this perspective was the beginning of forgiveness, healing, and changes in our parenting, as well as improved relationships with our children.

Doing the Simple Things Leads to the Joys of Spiritual Remembering

From this and many other experiences, I have learned that the best way to safeguard our relationships with loved ones is remembering our relationships and responsibilities to Heavenly Father and Jesus Christ and thereby experiencing the companionship of the Holy Ghost and the joys of the Savior's Atonement.

Remembering the Father and the Son means that our relationships with Them are more important than any other. Think of the time Jesus questioned Peter, saying, "Lovest thou me more than these?" (John 21:15 [15–17]). The Savior wasn't questioning whether His disciple loved the fish (or his profession) more than the sheep (or the Savior's flock). Jesus simply wanted him—and all of us—*to love Him and His Father more than anything else*. This is because when we love Them over everything else in our lives, *They* enable us to love our neighbor as ourselves (see Matthew 22:36–40). Through the power of His atoning sacrifice, Christ then cleanses our sins that weaken our relationships with others, He strengthens us to lift and help those we love, and He heals us from the effects of others' transgressions. Succoring us in our relationships with others is truly one of the greatest miracles of the Savior's Atonement!

Now, we understand that a loving and just God will never force us to love Him or to partake of the sweet fruit of His Son's sacrifice, but He knows there is a there is a "marked difference between having a taste of food and enjoying a continuing feast."[6] Heavenly Father yearns for us to remember our experiences with the Savior's cleansing, strengthening, and healing power so we that regularly obey His commands and offer a broken heart and a contrite spirit to be able to enjoy the sanctifying nourishment of Christ's sacrifice, as well as sweet relationships with each other.

Because "our greatest need is to remember," Spencer W. Kimball declared the word *remember* to be the most important one in the dictionary.[7] Spiritual remembering is more than a cerebral experience of reproducing information. It is something we do with our minds and our spirits. It not only merges our efforts to obey and to sacrifice, but it also increases our ability to believe in God's word, hearken to His Spirit, and honor sacred covenants to Him.

King Benjamin's instruction for spiritual remembering is first *what* to remember. He said, "remember, and always retain in remembrance, the greatness of God" (Mosiah 4:11), "the atonement which has been prepared from the foundation of the world" (Mosiah 4:6), and "[our] own nothingness" (Mosiah 4:11). This counsel is different than simply remembering one member of the Godhead. Remembering the love of the Father means we also seek the companionship of His Spirit and the grace of the Son. Becoming a disciple of Christ means we won't forget our Heavenly Father or His Holy Spirit. And remembering our nothingness means we won't forget our everlasting reliance on any of Them.

After teaching what to remember, King Benjamin then emphasized *how* to always remember so that we might always rejoice: "Humble yourselves even in the depths of humility, calling on the name of the Lord daily, and standing steadfastly in the faith of that which is to come" (Mosiah 4:11), or staying faithful to the conditions of obedience and sacrifice as set forth by the coming Lord (see Mosiah 4:6–11).

This ancient prophet's counsel of humility, prayer, and faithfulness to Christ provides easy ways to offer a broken heart and a contrite spirit in order to believe and to do. President Henry B. Eyring often linked spiritual remembering with doing the simple things,[8] for they always remind us of our need for Heavenly Father, Jesus Christ, and the Holy Ghost. The simple act of prayer helps us to submit our will to Heavenly Father and thus receive His Holy Spirit and the joys of the Son's Atonement. This is why the command to "remember always" is closely associated with the charge to "pray always." I believe Elder Richard G. Scott's address on acquiring spiritual guidance is the perfect way to always have a prayer in our hearts. He encouraged us to remember divine impressions by recording them, pondering our feelings associated with them, studying their meaning and application, thanking our Father for them, and then asking, "Was there yet more to be given?"[9]

The scriptures also help us remember our most critical relationships to Heavenly Father and His Son, as well as our mortal nothingness. Scriptures contain the mysteries of God and make it possible to "have his commandments always before our eyes" (Mosiah 1:5). Elder D. Todd Christofferson said "the scriptures enlarge our memory by helping us always to remember the Lord and our relationship to Him and the Father. They remind us of what we knew in our premortal life. And they expand our memory in another sense by teaching us about epochs, people, and events that we did not experience personally."[10]

By studying Nephi's Psalm, for example, we understand Nephi's struggles with the recent death of his father, the full weight of his prophetic mantle, and the imminent dangers posed by his unrepentant brothers. We see the anguish of Nephi's soul, for "when [he desired] to rejoice, [his] heart groaneth because of [his] sins" (2 Nephi 4:19). But we also learn from his example that he recalled miraculous times of protection, spiritual enlightenment, and divine guidance (see 2 Nephi 4:19–25). By likening these passages to our lives, we can remember the times when the Lord delivered us from physical and spiritual harm, the times our hearts were filled with His charity for those who were unkind, the times our cries were heard by Heavenly Father and we were given revelation by His Spirit, the times the Savior sent earthly angels to bless us with comfort and validation, and the times we received witnesses of truth too sacred to share with others. Remembering these grand blessings will always turn our hearts back to God, magnifying our resolve to be worthy of His Spirit and to gain the joys of His Son's Atonement. Thus, outside the scriptures, there is no other tangible object that has power to help us remember—and thus bring the Spirit and the fruit of God's love—every time we study its pages!

Delighting in the Sabbath and the Sacrament

One of the most simple and yet most significant means of spiritual remembering is the ordinance of the sacrament. Elder Russell M. Nelson taught that the Sabbath is a gift from the Savior, a "real respite from the rigors of daily life and an opportunity for spiritual and physical renewal."[11] More than a day of rest, it is time set aside to remember the goodness of God, the Atonement of His Son, and our dependence upon the members of the Godhead. As we truly "remember the sabbath day, to keep it holy" (Exodus 20:8), we will "call the sabbath a delight" (Isaiah 58:13).

When I was young, the sacrament was merely a break in the meeting. Though I knew I was supposed to be reverent, my mind often wandered until someone returned to the pulpit. It took me years to understand that although this ordinance is a time to pray and give thanks, its major purpose is to worship God—meaning we "come unto the Father in [the name of His Son]."[12] As we worship Heavenly Father, we reflect on our lives and recommit ourselves to Him and to His Son. Jeffrey R. Holland asked,

> Do we see [the sacrament] as *our* passover, remembrance of *our* safety and deliverance and redemption? With so very much at stake, this ordinance commemorating our escape from the angel of darkness should be taken more seriously than it sometimes is. It should be a powerful, reverent, reflective moment. It should encourage spiritual feelings and impressions. As such it should not be rushed. It is not something to "get over" so that the real purpose of a sacrament meeting can be pursued. This *is* the real purpose.[13]

As you recall, thinking about the sacrifice of the Savior powerfully influences our willingness to return to the basics of obedience and sacrifice, but ordinances and covenants drive our remembering and further our spiritual growth in a powerful way. As noted earlier, the fruit of the tree of life symbolizes the blessings of the Atonement, but "partaking of the fruit of the tree represents the receiving of ordinances and covenants whereby the Atonement can become fully efficacious in our lives."[14] Think of that! Because the sacrament is an ordinance associated with a sacred covenant, it not only helps us remember but it also unlocks the blessings of the Atonement in our lives! Every week, as we eat the bread in remembrance of the Savior's broken flesh and drink of the water in remembrance His blood, we are promised that we will "always have his Spirit to be with [us]" (D&C 20:77). The constant companionship of the Holy Ghost continues to draw us nearer unto Jesus Christ and His Father and enhances our ability to enjoy the blessings of obeying God's commandments and of offering a sacrifice of repentance, good works, and submission. Thus, *always having the Spirit* will guarantee *always rejoicing* in the joys of the Father, His Son, and the Holy Ghost.

In order to increase our joys on the Sabbath Day, we must do the simple things during the week to remember our reliance on Heavenly Father, His Only Begotten Son, and His Spirit. And we must come to the sacrament table, "hungering and thirsting for righteousness, for spiritual growth."[15] During sacrament meeting we can try something new to fuel our worship to God. For instance, instead of just singing the sacramental hymns, we can ponder their meaning and look for lyrics related to remembering the Father and His Son, as well as our dependence upon Them. As the sacramental prayers are being offered, we can repeat the words of the covenant in our minds and intentionally think about how we are doing in our efforts to take upon ourselves the name of Christ, to always remember Him and His Father, and to keep the commandments (see Moroni 4:3; D&C 20:77). While partaking of the sacrament, we can picture the Savior's suffering in Gethsemane and Golgotha, and we can imagine ourselves with the Nephites and ponder how it would change our lives to touch the hands and feet of the resurrected Lord.

Some time ago, I decided to try pondering and praying during the sacrament to understand how I needed to repent and become more like the Savior. On the first Sunday, I was quickly reminded of watching a movie that had been highly recommended by a trustworthy friend. As with a lot of movies, it had contained "just one bad scene." During the sacrament, the Spirit whispered that viewing *anything* sexually inappropriate—even if the message of the movie is inspiring—could be likened to viewing pornography, and I vowed I would never subject my family to it again.

My experiment during the sacrament continued for the next few months, and each Sabbath, I was given very specific direction, as well as the divine gift of forgiveness and strength to change and become better. One Sunday, I was prompted to remember that my involvement with two disagreeing friends had made things worse; and I was instructed that I should not speak for someone else—even if I thought I could help! The following week, I was reminded of Heavenly Father's awareness for me and I was given His loving reassurance in my ability to become more long-suffering with health challenges. The next time I took the sacrament, I remembered patting myself on the back for doing a good turn and was distinctively directed to purge pride from my life. And yet another week, I learned through the Spirit the reason for a chaotic and frustrating week and was urged to make family scriptures and prayers a priority again.

One Sunday as I entered the chapel, I felt an overwhelming excitement in knowing exactly how I needed to repent that week. My joy came from feeling that Heavenly Father was pleased with my efforts to analyze my life and my willingness to repent and change my behavior. Though I honestly sorrowed for my wrongs that week, I didn't feel humiliation. Rather, I was confident that Heavenly Father and His Son and His Spirit would do anything to help me receive and retain a remission of my sins and become faithful, hopeful, and charitable.

These weekly experiments changed the way I viewed my Sabbath worship and the sacrament's power to remember and reflect and renew. Truman G. Madsen taught that "in his sacrament—and in all the other ordinances—the Lord gives us glimpses of ourselves. In self-examination we are most blessed when we begin to see ourselves as we are seen by him and know ourselves as we are known by him (see D&C 76:94). [Just as] knowledge of the Savior and self-knowledge flow together,"[16] so the sacrament "does renew and symbolize the ongoing relationship by which Christ forgives, nourishes, and sustains us in all the turmoil of our lives."[17] Truly, as we learn of our imperfections, transgressions, and sins, and then as we exchange them for the sacramental emblems, the grace of God is effected in our lives and we are renewed—blessed and sanctified by His grace.

Remembering Cultivates Christlike Characteristics

As we think about *what* to remember—the goodness of God, the atoning sacrifice of Jesus Christ, and our own nothingness—and *how* to remember—through humble prayer, scripture study, and sacramental worship—we must never forget *why* we do the simple things. President Dieter F. Uchtdorf declared that "the 'what' and 'how' of obedience mark the way and keep us on the right path," but "the eternal fire and majesty of the gospel springs from the 'why.' When we understand *why* our Heavenly Father has given us this pattern for living, when we remember *why* we committed to making it a foundational part of our lives, the gospel ceases to become a burden and, instead, becomes a joy and a delight." God "wants us to become perfect," and becoming like Him and His Son is truly "the majesty, the beauty, and the exhilarating joy of the 'why' of the gospel of Jesus Christ"![18]

As we come unto Christ, we are "perfected in him" (Moroni 10:32). Perfection is a simply the process of steadily gaining His divine attributes as we remember and follow His teachings. "Largely through the medium of the Holy Ghost, our covenant-based and Atonement-based relationship with Christ goes on to bless us with the affirmative endowments of hope and charity, gifts that are extended and bestowed as Christ . . . guides and nourishes each of us toward a Christlike nature."[19] The following list briefly describes the cascading joys of spiritual remembering—the

Christlike attributes demanded in our discipleship to the Savior[20] and the characteristics that further bless our most important relationships with one another.

Faith and Knowledge. Because doing the simple things invites the Holy Ghost into our lives, the Spirit will "teach [us] all things, and bring all things to [our] remembrance" (John 14:26). As we are reminded of the truths learned long ago, our testimonies of truth will grow and our faith and trust in God will increase. King Benjamin explained it this way: If you always remember, "ye shall grow in the knowledge of the glory of him that created you, or in the knowledge that which is just and true" (Mosiah 4:12).

Spiritual Protection. With the constant companionship of the Holy Ghost, we also gain spiritual protection by relying on the Savior and His Father. President Eyring promised, "If you will let your heart be drawn to the Savior and always remember Him, and if you will draw near to our Heavenly Father in prayer, you will have put on spiritual armor. You will be protected against pride because you will know that any success comes not from your human powers. And you will be protected against the thoughts which come rushing in upon us that we are too weak, too inexperienced, too unworthy to do what we are called of God to do to serve and help save His children."[21]

Diligence and Virtue. Shielded from the adversary's fiery darts, we will keenly remember to obey God's commands and to repent often. Doing so will bring the great joys of "always [retaining] a remission of [our] sins" (Mosiah 4:12), which will eventually unlock the joys of keeping ourselves clean and "unspotted from the world" (D&C 59:9; see also D&C 59:7–8). The more we receive clean hands from the atoning grace of the Savior, the more we will realize the joys of a pure and virtuous heart. With Christ's help, "the penitent will then experience the sanctifying power of the Holy Ghost, which will fill them with peace of conscience and the joy of reconciliation with God. In a wondrous union of divine attributes, the same God who teaches us to walk with a broken heart invites us to rejoice and to be of good cheer."[22]

Gratitude. In this sanctifying process of discipleship, we will notice the tender mercies of God in our lives and gratefully "confess his hand in all things"[23] (see D&C 59:21). Elder Neil L. Andersen assured us that "seeing and believing the Lord's miracles in establishing His kingdom on earth can help us see and believe that the Lord's hand is at work in our own lives as well."[24] President Thomas S. Monson also taught that "sincerely giving thanks not only helps us recognize our blessings, but it also unlocks the doors of heaven and helps us feel God's love."[25]

Hope, Confidence, and Patience. Experiencing such gratitude leads us to glorious hope in God's plan of happiness. President Uchtdorf taught that in the gospel, hope is "not knowledge, but rather the abiding trust that the Lord will fulfill His promise to us. It is confidence that if we live according to God's laws and the words of His prophets now, we will receive desired blessings in the future,"[26] "even peace in this world, and eternal life in the world to come" (D&C 59:23). As we are willing to believe in His promises and expect that our prayers will be answered, we are also more likely to be willing to do God's will with "confidence, optimism, enthusiasm, and patient perseverance."[27]

Charity and Love. Joyful expectations for our future will reinforce our understanding of God's love for us, and in turn, we will receive the crowning reward of remembering—to "be filled with the love of God" (Mosiah 4:12) for our neighbors, family members, and even strangers. Though most people define charity as simply giving to those in need, Latter-day Saints also equate charity with the "highest, noblest, and strongest kind of love"[29] that the Savior has for us and that we should have for each other. Through spiritual remembering, we will live as a "complete Christian," one who "will have no mind to injure, will live peaceably, will render to others justly, and will care for his or her children, also teaching them to love and to serve one another and to succor the needy"[28] (see Mosiah 4:12–16).

Because "the best and most clear indicator that we are progressing spiritually and coming unto Christ is the way we treat other people,"[30] we can see that becoming Christlike is at the heart of our relationships. Christlike virtues—especially the pure love of Christ—help us understand the responsibilities required in our most significant earthly relationships. As we remember Him and His Father, the Savior distinguishes pride, criticisms, and contention from our hearts and fills them with deeper levels of trust, forgiveness, communication, acceptance, appreciation, empathy, and loyalty. As this happens, we will more likely stand for righteousness and expect virtuous and honorable behaviors from those around us. With specific direction from the Spirit, we will be given strength to mend relationships that need to be fixed, to distance ourselves from those that don't need to be fixed, and to eliminate abusive and harmful relationships altogether.[31]

The bottom line of remembering is this: "By small and simple things are great things brought to pass" (Alma 37:6)! I testify that remembering the goodness of God, the sacrifice of the Son, and our own nothingness is precisely what we need to do to become as the Savior and to find and keep His joy. Consistent prayers, scripture study, and Sabbath worship remind us of our responsibilities of obedience and sacrifice and bless us with the precious fruit of the Savior's Atonement and the subsequent blessings of becoming more Christlike in thought, word, and deed. Ultimately, remembering brings heaven-sent joy. It enriches our relationship with Heavenly Father, our discipleship to the Savior, and our relationships with our loved ones.

May we recommit again and again to King Benjamin's prescribed pathway of joy, for obedience, sacrifice, and remembering will lead to the "exquisite and sweet" joys of spiritual rebirth (Alma 36:21; see also Alma 36:22–23), as well as the grand and marvelous opportunities of discipleship to Christ.

Notes

1. Terryl Givens and Fiona Givens, *The God Who Weeps: How Mormonism Makes Sense of Life* (Salt Lake City: Ensign Peak, 2012), 109.
2. "Every Family Has a Story—Discover Yours," Mormon.org, accessed August 8, 2014, www.mormon.org/blog/family-history-genealogy-your-story.
3. Givens and Givens, *The God Who Weeps*, 113.
4. "The Family: A Proclamation to the World," *Ensign*, November 2010.
5. Henry B. Eyring, "That We May Be One," *Ensign*, May 1998.
6. Susan Easton Black, "King Benjamin: In the Service of Your God," in Monte S. Nyman and Charles D. Tate Jr., eds., *The Book of Mormon: Mosiah, Salvation Only through Christ* (Provo, UT: Religious Studies Center, 1991), 43.
7. Spencer W. Kimball, "Circles of Exaltation" (address to Church Educational System religious educators, June 28, 1968), 5.

8. See Henry B. Eyring, "Always," *Ensign*, October 1999; see also "In the Strength of the Lord," *Ensign*, May 2004; "O Remember, Remember," *Ensign*, November 2007; "Act in All Diligence," *Ensign*, May 2010.
9. Richard G. Scott, "To Acquire Spiritual Guidance," *Ensign*, November 2009.
10. D. Todd Christofferson, "The Blessings of Scripture," *Ensign*, May 2010.
11. Russell M. Nelson, "The Sabbath Is a Delight," *Ensign*, May 2015.
12. Truman G. Madsen, *The Temple: Where Heaven Meets Earth* (Salt Lake City: Deseret Book, 2008), 19.
13. Jeffrey R. Holland, "'This Do in Remembrance of Me,'" *Ensign*, November 1995; emphasis in original.
14. David A. Bednar, "Lehi's Dream: Holding Fast to the Iron Rod," *Ensign*, October 2011.
15. Melvin J. Ballard, "Classic Discourses from the General Authorities: The Sacramental Covenant," *New Era*, January 1976.
16. Truman G. Madsen, *Sacramental Reflections: Feasting at the Lord's Table* (Salt Lake City: Deseret Book, 2015), 35.
17. Bruce C. Hafen and Marie K. Hafen, *The Belonging Heart: The Atonement and Relationships with God and Family* (Salt Lake City: Deseret Book, 1994), 146.
18. Dieter F. Uchtdorf, "Forget Me Not," *Ensign*, November 2011; emphasis in original.
19. Hafen and Hafen, *The Belonging* Heart, 153.
20. Elder Neal A. Maxwell taught, "We can begin to sense the specific demands of discipleship in terms of the virtues Benjamin encourages his listeners to develop: meekness, humility, patience, love, spiritual submissiveness." ("King Benjamin's Manual of Discipleship," *Ensign*, January 1992.) See also "How Do I Develop Christlike Attributes?" in *Preach My Gospel: A Guide to Missionary Service* (2004), 115–26.
21. Eyring, "Always."
22. Bruce D. Porter, "A Broken Heart and a Contrite Spirit," *Ensign*, November 2007.
23. Ezra Taft Benson, "Pray Always," *Ensign*, February 1990.
24. Neil L. Andersen, "Thy Kingdom Come," *Ensign*, May 2015.

25. Thomas S. Monson, "The Divine Gift of Gratitude," *Ensign*, November 2010.
26. Dieter F. Uchtdorf, "The Infinite Power of Hope," *Ensign*, November 2008.
27. Ibid.
28. Maxwell, "King Benjamin's Manual of Discipleship."
29. "Charity," Gospel Topics, topics.lds.org.
30. Marvin J. Ashton, "The Tongue Can Be a Sharp Sword," *Ensign*, May 1992. President Russell M. Nelson also taught that "every time we nurture our spouse and guide our children, every time we forgive someone or ask for forgiveness, we can feel joy" ("Joy and Spiritual Survival," *Ensign*, November 2016.)
31. *Handbook 2: Administering the Church (2010)*, 21.4.2 states, "The Church's position is that abuse cannot be tolerated in any form. Those who abuse or are cruel to their spouses, children, other family members, or anyone else violate the laws of God and man. All members, especially parents and leaders, are encouraged to be alert and diligent and do all they can to protect children and others against abuse and neglect. Members who have abused others are subject to Church discipline." See also Richard G. Scott, "Healing the Tragic Scars of Abuse," *Ensign*, May 1992.

4: *Rejoice* and Cleave unto Thy Covenants

The experiences of one of my ancestors helped me understand how discovering the joys of the Savior occur as we are converted to Christ through a process of spiritual transformation. Mary was born in England in 1907. With an Irish Catholic father and a British Methodist mother, her home life was anything but religious. When Mary was sixteen years old, her mother joined the LDS Church, and Mary was baptized at a neighboring bathhouse months later. After learning more about the gospel for almost two years, she met her future husband, William, while he was serving in her branch as a full-time missionary. After his faithful service, William returned home and spent two years encouraging Mary to immigrate to the United States. In the end, she chose to leave behind everything she loved—her family, her posh job, and her supportive network of the small English branch—to join the Saints in Utah.

Coming to Zion, however, was not what it was cracked up to be. After an arduous two-week journey, Mary experienced unexpected culture shock and great disappointment. The lush green rolling hills of England compared to the dry desert weeds of Utah were one thing, but the worst part of Mary's arrival was discovering that her future in-laws all wished William would marry a local girl instead! Yet love prevailed, and six weeks later, the two were sealed in the Salt Lake Temple. The newlyweds moved to a small duplex near the train tracks. William left early each morning to work on his father's farm, and Mary spent the day alone until he returned at night. This was the beginning of the most lonesome part of her life, and she later said if the ocean hadn't separated her from her family and friends, she would have walked home!

After a year, Mary and William moved to his father's farm. But with the Great Depression in full swing, all they could afford was a two-room wooden shack with no insulation under the floorboards. They lived off the land, eating hash browns, potato salad, potato soup, and baked, mashed, fried, and cubed potatoes. The economy, a severe drought, and years of pestilence financially crippled William, and he lost most of his land to foreclosure. Mary said it was physically and mentally painful to get through each day. Yet, while she was attending church, she discovered she didn't worry about her burdens. Honoring covenants gave her strength to endure and courage to accept a calling to teach children and to begin genealogy for her family.

After the Depression, three of Mary's four children contracted polio. During this divine tutorial, she and William experienced many tender mercies. Mary met a nurse trained in "hot packing" and then she worked tirelessly to apply heat to keep the muscles pliable in the children's afflicted limbs. Mary then contracted the dreaded disease and could hardly swallow. With a priesthood blessing from William, she was miraculously healed just after the consecrated oil was returned to its cupboard. After one of their sons was hospitalized, his throat became so swollen with infection that the doctors were sure he wouldn't live. Though William began to lose hope, Mary received an impression from the Spirit that their son would be all right. At the very time they prayed for him at home, their son asked for a drink at the hospital. This was the beginning of his recovery. Mary convinced the doctors she could do more for her son at home. He returned to his family and spent the next eight months lying on the kitchen table, receiving hot packing treatments, and thereby escaping paralysis and other disabilities.

Mary knew God had preserved their children's lives. Healing and divine strength not only solidified her testimony of the goodness of God and the enabling power of the Son, but they also became the foundation of her relationship with God and a deep commitment in bringing others unto Christ. Line upon line, her very nature blossomed with Christlike virtues, and she became undeniably happy and radiant and joyful, spending the remainder of her life in selfless service.

Now, it would be hard to pin point the exact time when Mary's heart was changed and she had "no more desire to do evil" (Alma 19:33). Her initial experiences of faith and repentance formed the basis of her testimony and led her to the spiritual rebirth of baptism. Keeping covenants further qualified her for the companionship of the Spirit and led her to the ordinances of the temple. Each spiritual experience built upon another, gradually changing her from the natural man to "a state of righteousness" (Mosiah 27:25). She was transformed and converted "step by step, degree by degree, level by level, from a lower state to a higher, from grace to grace, until the time that [she was] wholly turned to the cause of righteousness."[1]

The Sweet Transformation of Spiritual Rebirth

For Mary and for each of us, we come unto Christ and become like Him through spiritual rebirth. Like discipleship, rebirth begins with baptism when we take upon ourselves the name of Christ. Yet baptism "alone does *not* constitute the spiritual rebirth that allows us to return to the presence of Heavenly Father."[2] Spiritual rebirth must continue with the "baptism of fire," or the sanctifying process of receiving the continuous fruit of the Atonement and thus receiving the Spirit, who "erases carnality and brings us into a state of righteousness."[3] For most of us, this rebirth is usually a lifelong endeavor of becoming fully converted to the cause of Christ, rather than simply gaining a testimony of Him.[4]

Though King Benjamin had helped his people gain a witness of the goodness of God, the power of the Savior's Atonement, and their own nothingness, his ultimate goal was to "effect a 'change in heart' in his people and to bring them to Jesus Christ."[5] These Nephites were moved by the reception of the Spirit to a new spiritual plateau, one of increased trust in and commitment to God. With greater faith and willingness to obey and to sacrifice for His cause, they cried with one voice, proclaiming belief in all the words of their king and exclaiming that the "Spirit of the Lord Omnipotent [had] wrought a mighty change in [them], or in [their] hearts, that [they had] no more disposition to do evil, but to do good continually" (Mosiah 5:2). Perhaps for many of these Saints, this change of heart was the first day of serious discipleship to the Master.

Further sensing more than ever their everlasting potential and joy, these Saints exclaimed, "Through the infinite goodness of God, and the manifestations of his Spirit, [we] have great views of that which is to come; and were it expedient, we could prophesy of all things" (Mosiah 5:3; see also Mosiah 5:2–4). Now, the kind of faith to prophesy of all things and to rejoice with such exceedingly great joy suggests more than just increased piety to the law of Moses. It was great hope and expectation for the future. It was optimism, confidence, fortitude, and excitement. It was joy on a grand scale!

Experiencing such glorious feelings and eternal perspective, King Benjamin's people desired to preserve their heartfelt change by "[entering] into a covenant with [their] God to do his will, and to be obedient to his commandments in all things that he [would] command [them], all the remainder of [their] days" (Mosiah 5:5). Stephen D. Ricks asserts that King Benjamin carefully followed practices similar to ancient "covenant renewal festivals" held in Old Testament times. As part of these ceremonies, the leader "[cut] the covenant" and the participants collectively reaffirmed or reestablished their baptismal covenants with God.[6]

Once this sacred promise had been offered by the entire group, King Benjamin pointed out that "because of the covenant which ye have made ye shall be called the children of Christ, his sons, and his daughters; for behold, this day he hath spiritually begotten you" (Mosiah 5:7).

From this miraculous account, we can conclude a couple of things. First, experiencing a mighty change of heart is a fundamental turning point of one's spiritual rebirth or discipleship to Christ. Second, we can also surmise that taking upon ourselves the name of Christ and becoming His children through priesthood ordinances and covenants—the culmination of King Benjamin's address—is the pinnacle of gaining the Savior's joys and coming unto the Father.

The Joys of Taking Christ's Name through Temple Ordinances

The Prophet Joseph taught that "being born again, comes by the Spirit of God through ordinances."[7] This means that our spiritual rebirth is broadened and expanded as we take upon ourselves the name of Christ through formal priesthood ordinances and covenants. "These start with baptism and conclude with temple covenants, with many others, such as partaking of the sacrament, laced throughout our lives as additional blessings and reminders."[8]

Dallin H. Oaks taught that we fully take upon ourselves the name of Christ through the crowning ordinances and covenants of the temple.[9] While every temple is magnificent in its specific design and splendor, the Savior's joy from temples has more to do with what happens because we go there. Here is a sample of the marvelous rejoicing we can discover within the temple.

The temple is a place of *peace* and *prayer*. Temples are dedicated as holy sanctuaries where we can find peace through "a closeness to God that comes through consistent worship"[10] and "a wonderfully rich communion with God" through His Spirit.[11] Our relationship to our Heavenly Father can be nurtured in the temple. "Sometimes in the temple we feel like we are praying in the Garden of Eden and life is all beauty and goodness. And sometimes it is as if we are praying in the Garden of Gethsemane, and it is too hard to bear." Either way, "the temple is a retreat and a place of Christ's intensive care, where His rays come together in focus and peace."[12]

The temple is a place of *priesthood ordinances and covenants*. In order to return to God's presence, He has commanded that we build temples and participate in priesthood ordinances and covenants. An "ordinance is a sacred formal act performed by the authority of the priesthood."[13] An ordinance is also "an earthly symbol [of] a covenant or agreement with the Lord."[14] Like the act of immersion at baptism, the ordinances of the temple endowment are associated with sacred covenants to live a Christlike life. President Russell M. Nelson explained that "the basis for every temple ordinance and covenant—the heart of the plan of salvation—is the Atonement of Jesus Christ."[15] As with baptism, temple ordinances are "also 'a similitude of the Only Begotten,'" helping us offer ourselves to Him and thus "receive the blessings of His blessed offering."[16]

The temple is a place of *perspective*. Our Heavenly Father loves us and knows "it is extremely important that we do not make decisions of eternal value from the perspective of mortality."[17] Participation in temple ordinances and covenants brings eternal perspective, and gaining perspective is part of the "quickening process of the temple."[18] In the temple, "we are taught about the purpose of life, the mission and Atonement of Jesus Christ, and Heavenly Father's plan for His children. We gain a glimpse of what it will be like to live in His presence as we feel the peaceful atmosphere of the temple."[19]

The temple is a place of *personal revelation.* In the Lord's "house of learning" (D&C 109:8), Heavenly Father endows or enriches us with "wisdom and great treasures of knowledge, even hidden treasures" (D&C 89:19). New insights regarding God's greatness and goodness and the Son's Atonement then become the "catalyst whereby the self is revealed to the self."[20] Revelation thus deepens our relationship with Heavenly Father and helps us become a better disciple of Christ. In the temple we may find "all the Lord's answers," many of which include answers to "practical, very realistic, down-to-earth problems."[21] We "can take our deepest concerns . . . and spread them before the Lord and expect to come away lightened in both senses of the word: no longer carrying burdens of care and with an understanding of the course we should take."[22]

The temple is a place of *power and protection.* Building upon the preparatory ordinances of the Aaronic Priesthood, we are "taught from on high" and endowed "with power from on high" (D&C 43:16; 95:8) in the temple. The Melchizedek Priesthood not only holds "the key of the mysteries of the kingdom, even the key of the knowledge of God," but it also manifests "the power of godliness" in the ordinances it officiates (D&C 84:19–20). Through these ordinances, we become more godlike, shielded from the adversary's persuasions and blessed to keep our covenants. Temple "keys and insights . . . can enable us to live a godly life in a very worldly world, protected—yes, even insulated—from the poisons and distortions that are everywhere."[23] The temple thus becomes "a fortress—there we withdraw from the world in order to return fortified to the struggle."[24]

The temple is a place of *preparation* and *purification.* Especially in the temple, "true doctrine, understood, changes attitudes and behavior."[25] President David O. McKay said there are few people who "comprehend the full meaning and power of the temple endowment. Seen for what it is, it is a step-by-step ascent into the Eternal Presence."[26] Partaking of the fruit of the Atonement through temple worship "is absolutely necessary" in preparing us for eternal life and making us whole like the Savior—helping us move "from grace to grace to become more and more."[27] Truly, this "holy precinct" helps us "walk out of the world . . . and feel the glorious difference, and then reenter the world with the determination to keep the holiness with us."[28]

The temple is a place of *prelude*, or as Joseph Smith said, "a prelude of those joys that God will pour out on that day." While the Prophet was referring to receiving the promised endowment, we can also conclude that the joys in the temple are but a prelude of the joys of exaltation.[29] Because our future joys include being reunited with our loved ones, President Ezra Taft Benson proclaimed that "the temple is an ever-present reminder that God intends the family to be eternal."[30] There is "resilient joy in the temple," for it is the only place where the keys and glory of "an even richer quality of love" are available both to receive for ourselves and to give to others. Thus, "only in the temple are [we] placed in covenant-harmony with divine powers which will eventually so infuse and fuse [our] love that it will be worth perpetuating forever." Indeed, the temple is "where Christ's atonement manifests to us the 'peaceable things—that which bringest joy, that which bringeth life eternal' (D&C 42:61). To miss the joy is to miss the point."[31]

The Joys of Retaining the Savior's Name through Covenant Keeping

As you can guess, taking upon the name of the Savior through ordinances is critical to our discipleship, but retaining His name is just as essential. This is because "receiving sacred ordinances without accepting and keeping associated covenants is living a religion of appearances—'having a form of godliness; but denying the power thereof' (2 Timothy 3:5[])". We only claim "the power and the promised blessings" by "keeping the covenants."[32] Truly, divine direction, redemption, and sanctification "are a result of living on the covenant path."[33]

We know that staying on the path of discipleship isn't always easy, yet our most oft-quoted scripture about joy—"Men are, that they might have joy"—is found in the same chapter as our most oft-quoted verse on opposition: "For it must needs be, that there is an opposition in all things" (2 Nephi 2:25, 11). The placement of these two is not by chance, for the great plan of happiness is achieved only through faithfulness at all times and in all places and in all situations. Most of the accounts in the Book of Mormon describe individuals entangled in family contentions, bloody battles, and spiritual controversy. These scriptural accounts were preserved for us so that we can understand how to claim the Savior's joy—even during the most difficult times. Consider the following truths I have learned about covenant keeping, opposition, and joy.

Truth #1: The absence of joy does not always equate to lack of righteousness. Once while preparing a lesson on the joys of womanhood, I was inspired to call a struggling friend. After talking for over an hour, I was prompted to call others who were weary in their own afflictions. One long and tender phone call followed another, and soon the day was gone. When I related this to my husband, I felt frustration that a day of service hadn't resulted in rejoicing. Instead, a heavy weight of sorrow hung over me. I mourned for dear friends with constant, complicated, and presumably insolvable problems. After much pondering and praying about this situation, I received the strong witness that Heavenly Father did *not* want me to preach: "Just try harder and you'll have joy!" Even while keeping our covenants, we still cannot avoid all of life's inconsistencies and inconveniences, Satan's deceptions, and others' imperfections and poor choices. Even the most joyful transitions in life—that of receiving a new calling, getting married, starting a new job, becoming a parent, and so on—will take us out of our comfort zone and compel us to expend our efforts in soul searching and heaven reaching. Precisely during these times, we must be drawn again and again to the altar of the sacrament table and the ordinances of the temple. We then can receive the Lord's strength to be sustained to keep our covenants.

Truth #2: It is possible to simultaneously experience intense joy and overwhelming sorrow. Though we don't always feel joy during difficult seasons, it is possible to experience even intense joy and intense sorrow at the same time. I learned this truth years ago while encountering tremendous health challenges. Though I couldn't have predicted it, this difficult season also coincided with my initial quest to understand and attain more joy in life. While searching for answers to my personal needs, I was similarly enriched with many spiritual insights about joy. These revelations brought me immense joy—even during the times of overwhelming frustration. Since then, I have realized anew that always retaining the Savior's name qualifies us for the blessings of the Spirit—which is why one can experience joy even in the midst of overpowering sorrow. In fact, my greatest heroes are those who "have learned to suffer with joy,"[34] meaning those who serenely and patiently emulate the Savior, despite serious and debilitating afflictions.

Truth #3: "Joy has little to do with the circumstances of our lives and everything to do with the focus of our lives."[35] Elder Richard G. Scott explained that "sadness, disappointment, and severe challenge are *events* in life, not life itself" and "they should not be allowed to become the confining center of everything [we] do."[36] Mortality is meant to be filled with the Savior's redemption and His joy as much and as often as possible. President Russell M. Nelson promised, "When the focus of our lives is on God's plan of salvation . . . and Jesus Christ and His gospel, we can feel joy regardless of what is happening—or not happening—in our lives." We claim His joy by looking to Christ "in every thought" (D&C 6:36), by giving thanks for Him in our prayers, by honoring sacred covenants, and by "[pleading] for His joy to be given to us."[37]

Truth #4: Joy in adversity occurs as we are becoming Christlike. While participating in a youth handcart trek at Martin's Cove, I was surprised when a senior missionary said that he hoped our group would find joy in our stay. I wasn't prepared to rejoice in such a tragic, yet holy place. Hiking into the cove where the Saints had endured such tragedy, our group experienced their own hardships of blistered feet, severe heatstroke, and unsettling calls from home. I knew that in comparison to the suffering of the pioneers, these trials were nothing. But, all the same, I silently wished the journey to and from this sacred spot had included some element of joy.

When our ward gathered for testimony meeting the following night, I felt a twinge of disappointment and still wondered, *How can anyone rejoice in such a seemingly God-forsaken place*? Yet as the youth stood to bear their testimonies, I was overcome with the impression that everyone had felt the Spirit and experienced a life-changing witness of the love of God on our trip. I then knew nothing could possibly bring more joy than seeing others grow in their conversion to the Savior, and I stood and testified that adversity and joy are connected when we are becoming more like Christ. For the pioneers and the youth who had visited Martin's Cove, each had become more compassionate, serviceable, charitable, meek, long-suffering, and faithful. Truly, no other form of worldly pleasure can come close to the joy of having the Savior's name written in our hearts and being purified through His atoning blood.

God Trusts His Covenant People to Act in the Name of His Son

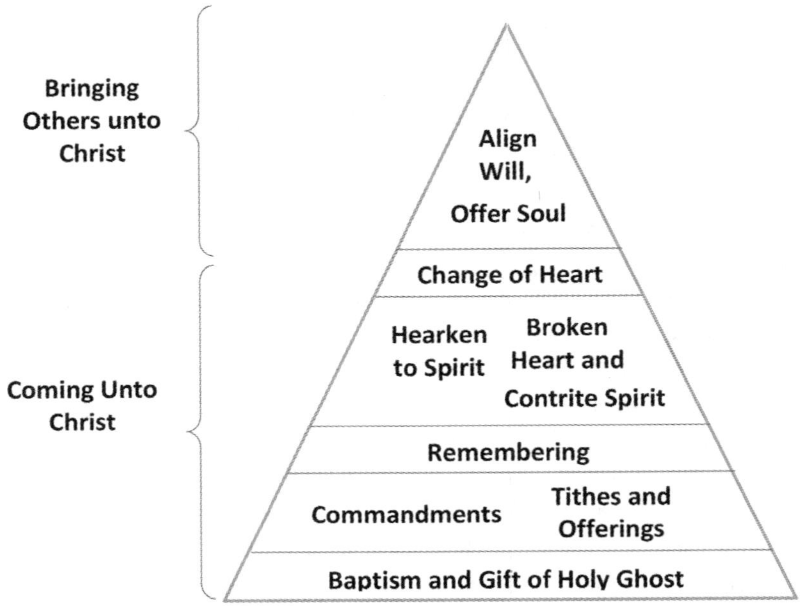

Now, given all we have discussed about the joys of coming unto Christ and being perfected in Him, you may be surprised to know that these are only the beginning of the supreme joys reserved for disciples of the Master.

The Savior's greatest joys come from bringing others unto Him. The whole reason for covenant making and covenant keeping is so that the Savior can first turn "every one of [us] from [our] iniquities" and then help us fulfill the Abrahamic covenant to bless the kindreds of the earth with the knowledge of His redemption (3 Nephi 20:26 [25–29]).

God made promises to Abraham and his seed, including the blessings of baptism ("the covenant of salvation"), the higher priesthood, celestial marriage ("the covenant of exaltation"), the assurance of eternal increase, and the offering of these same blessings to his posterity. In return, Abraham's promise was to take the gospel to all nations. After Moses and Elias appeared in the Kirtland Temple in 1836, Joseph Smith was given the same great commission to "bear the ministry and the priesthood unto all nations, so that all the families of the earth would be blessed with the gospel, salvation and life eternal."[38]

To help us understand our part of the Abrahamic covenant, Sister Bonnie Oscarson said, "God accomplishes His work through covenants. . . . God invites us to come out of our worldly sphere through covenants. We are invited to join Him, to partner with Him in our salvation and in the salvation of all of His children."[39] At baptism, we took upon us Christ's name by covenant. Bearing His name as Christians, we offer a broken heart and a contrite spirit to be willing to believe in Him and to act in His name and do the work of His kingdom.[40] Like Adam and Eve, we are commanded to "do all that thou doest in the name of the Son" (Moses 5:8). We repent and call upon God in His name to become converted unto Him, but in order to strengthen our brethren (Luke 22:32), we "must seek to think and speak and act as though we were the One whose blessed name we bear, so that our words and acts may become his words and acts."[41]

Acting in His name, the Lord's covenant people of all former dispensations have anticipated the fulfillment of the "new and everlasting covenant." This covenant simply means "the gospel of Jesus Christ" or "the sum of all gospel covenants that God makes with mankind."[42] The joyful news of our dispensation—the dispensation of the fulness of times—is that the promises of the new and everlasting covenant will be fulfilled and "the forces of righteousness will finally win."[43] While each of the former dispensations ended with apostasy and darkness, ours will not. Elder Jeffrey R. Holland asserted that "those great men and women, the leaders in those ages past, were able to keep going, to keep testifying, to keep trying to do their best, not because they knew that *they* would succeed but because they knew that *you* would."[44] Of this great truth, the Prophet Joseph—he who helped restore the new and everlasting covenant—prophesied,

> The Standard of Truth has been erected; no unhallowed hand can stop the work from progressing; persecutions may rage, mobs may combine, armies may assemble, calumny may defame, but the truth of God will go forth boldly, nobly, and independent, till it has penetrated every continent, visited every clime, swept every country, and sounded in every ear,

> till the purposes of God shall be accomplished, and the Great Jehovah shall say the work is done.[45]

In this last dispensation, you and I and each member of the restored Church of Jesus Christ—the vehicle for the fulfillment of this covenant—have the duty and numerous opportunities to further His work on the earth. We can and must help fulfill the promises of the new and everlasting covenant and "*prepare the Church of the Lamb of God to receive the Lamb of God*—in person, in triumphant glory, in His millennial role as Lord of Lord and King of Kings."[46]

Our Heavenly Father, the most powerful and omniscient Being of the universe, not only wants us to return to Him but also has confidence in our ability to assist with His great work and glory! He sent His Only Begotten Son to guide us through our spiritual rebirth—a process that starts with taking upon the name of Christ through ordinances and continues as we retain that name through covenant keeping and acting in His name to build up His kingdom. Because "taking our covenants seriously transforms us,"[47] I urge everyone, everywhere, to "lift up thy heart and rejoice, and cleave unto the covenants which thou hast made" (D&C 25:13). Being "steadfast and immovable, always abounding in good works" to bring others unto Christ is the way—the only way—for the "Lord God Omnipotent . . . [to] seal [us] his," for that is how we gain the joys of the Savior, how we "may be brought to heaven, [and how we] may have everlasting salvation and eternal life" (Mosiah 5:15).

Notes

1. Bruce R. McConkie, "Be Ye Converted," *Brigham Young University Speeches of the Year* (February 11, 1968), 12.
2. Keith K. Hilbig, "Experiencing a Change of Heart," *Ensign*, June 2008; emphasis in original.
3. Bruce R. McConkie, *A New Witness for the Articles of Faith* (Salt Lake City: Deseret Book, 1985), 290.
4. David E. Bednar teaches: "For many of us, conversion is an ongoing process and not a onetime event that results from a powerful or dramatic experience." ("Converted Unto the Lord," *Ensign* November 2012.)

5. Stephen D. Ricks, "Benjamin," in Daniel H. Ludlow, ed., *Encyclopedia of Mormonism: The History, Scripture, Doctrine, and Procedure of The Church of Jesus Christ of Latter-day Saints*, vol. 1 (New York: Macmillan, 1992), 99.
6. See Stephen D. Ricks, "The Treaty/Covenant Pattern in King Benjamin's Address (Mosiah 1–6)," *BYU Studies Quarterly* 24, no. 2 (1984), 151–62.
7. *Teachings of Presidents of the Church: Joseph Smith* (2007), 95.
8. Jeffrey R. Holland, "Broken Things to Mend," *Ensign*, May 2006.
9. See Dallin H. Oaks, "Taking upon Us the Name of Christ," *Ensign*, May 1985.
10. David E. Sorenson, "Small Temples—Large Blessings," *Ensign*, November 1998.
11. John A. Widtsoe, "Temple Worship," *The Utah Genealogical and Historical Magazine* 12 (1921): 56.
12. Truman G. Madsen, *The Temple: Where Heaven Meets Earth* (Salt Lake City: Deseret Book, 2008), 62.
13. "Ordinances," Gospel Topics, topics.lds.org.
14. John A. Widtsoe, comp., *Priesthood and Church Government* (Salt Lake City: Deseret Book, 1939), 348.
15. Russell M. Nelson, "Personal Preparation for Temple Blessings," *Ensign*, May 2001.
16. Bruce C. Hafen and Marie K. Hafen, *The Contrite Spirit: How the Temple Helps Us Apply Christ's Atonement* (Salt Lake City: Deseret Book, 2015), 64.
17. Rafael E. Pino, "The Eternal Perspective of the Gospel," *Ensign*, May 2015.
18. Madsen, *The Temple*, 48.
19. "Commonly Asked Questions," *Ensign*, October 2010.
20. Madsen, *The Temple*, 6.
21. Ibid., viii, 5.
22. Ibid., 60.
23. Ibid., 10.
24. Ibid., 92.

25. Boyd K. Packer, "Little Children," *Ensign*, November 1986.
26. Madsen, *The Temple*, 11.
27. Ibid., 75.
28. Ibid., 63.
29. Joseph Fielding Smith, *Teachings of the Prophet Joseph Smith* (Salt Lake City: Deseret Book, 1977), 91.
30. Ezra Taft Benson, "What I Hope You Will Teach Your Children about the Temple," *Ensign*, August 1985.
31. Madsen, *The Temple,* 96, ix.
32. Wilford W. Andersen, "Receiving and Retaining a Mighty Change," *Ensign,* April 2012.
33. "Your Covenant Path," in www.lds.org/youth/article/your-covenant-path?lang=eng; accessed 22 December 2016.
34. Russell M. Nelson, "Joy and Spiritual Survival," *Ensign*, November 2016.
35. Ibid.
36. Richard G. Scott, "Finding Joy in Life," *Ensign*, May 1996; emphasis in original.
37. Nelson, "Joy and Spiritual Survival."
38. See "A blessed people," *Church News* (June 28, 2008): 16.
39. Sarah Jane Weaver, "Love and Serve Others to Honor Covenants with God, Sister Oscarson Says," *Church News* (May 1, 2015). Bonnie Oscarson, in www.lds.org/church/news/love-and-serve-others-to-honor-covenants-with-god-sister-oscarson-says-?lang=eng; accessed 20 August 2015.
40. Elder Dallin H. Oaks said, "By witnessing our willingness to take upon us the name of Jesus Christ, we signify our willingness to do the work of his kingdom. ("Taking upon Us the Name of Jesus Christ," *Ensign*, May 1985.)
41. Robert L. Millet, "Honoring His Holy Name," *Ensign,* March 1994; see also Luke 22:32.
42. Cecil D. Clark, "New and Everlasting Covenant," in *Encyclopedia of Mormonism,* 3:1008.
43. Ezra Taft Benson, as quoted in Marvin J. Ashton, "'Stalwart and Brave We Stand'," *Ensign,* November 1989.

44. Jeffrey R. Holland, *Broken Things to Mend* (Salt Lake City: Deseret Book, 2008), 91–93.

45. Joseph Smith, in B. H. Roberts, *History of the Church of Jesus Christ of Latter-day Saints* (Salt Lake City: Deseret Book, 1976), 4:540.

46. Holland, *Broken Things to Mend,* 93; emphasis in original.

47. Madsen, *The Temple*, 57.

5: The *Joyful* Life of a Serious Disciple

One of my greatest seasons of experiencing the Savior's joy occurred while striving to bring others the gospel in Taiwan. Though this missionary work was exhausting, I felt moments of great joy all along the way. One of my favorite memories was preparing a wonderful young woman to take upon the yoke of Christ through baptism. Mo-Li had studied with other missionaries, but her family's Buddhist traditions often stood as a stumbling block to her commitment to the Lord. What's more, the closer Mo-Li got to her baptismal interview, the greater the pressure she felt to change her mind.

A week before her scheduled meeting, my companion and I spent almost four hours trying to resolve Mo-Li's fears about mysterious events happening in her home. Her family's Buddhist worship stand had fallen down and broken into pieces—a bad omen to her superstitious grandmother and mother, and a question as to whether Mo-Li should join our Church. The gods at the Buddhist temple had also been asked if her father should be given the responsibility to collect donations from his neighbors throughout the following year. The two divination or moon blocks had been thrown eight times, and each time the answer had been unbelievably affirmative. Mo-Li's family was upset about his new assignment because they knew it would add stress to the families' finances. And, as her family was doing all they could to please their gods, Mo-Li knew that her joining a Christian church would be viewed as bad luck.

We explained to Mo-Li that "all things which are good cometh of God" (Moroni 7:12), reassuring her that God gives us answers through His Spirit—not through other mediums—and that the ordinance of baptism was a joyful occasion. As Heavenly Father only wanted her happiness, we told her we would not pressure her to get baptized—the decision was completely hers. The following week, we were delighted when Mo-Li asked us to reschedule her baptismal interview. And days later, she entered the waters of baptism and emerged with peace, radiance, and joy! My companion and I also rejoiced, completely satisfied that she would be able to receive the gift of the Holy Ghost herself. It was a day of great rejoicing for everyone!

To accept the Savior's invitation to bring others unto Him is to participate in some of the most exciting and joyous work upon the earth. We act in name of Christ through service and we discover His joy through growing relationships with those whom we serve.

In the premortal realm, we agreed "to be not only saviors for ourselves but . . . saviors for the whole human family. We went into a partnership with the Lord. The working out of the plan became then not merely the Father's work, and the Savior's work, but also our work."[1] If we labor all our days and bring even one soul unto Him, "how great shall be [our] joy with him in the kingdom of [His] Father!" (D&C 18:15 [15–16]). Though we typically use this verse to discuss the inexpressible joys of missionary work, we will discover this same great joy helping any of God's children on the covenant path to the Savior.

D. Todd Christofferson asserted that the world needs "strong Christians . . . who can lift others by their example and their compassion" and those "who can defend the truth of Jesus Christ against moral relativism and militant atheism."[2] Obviously, we of the Latter-day faith haven't cornered the market on the Savior's grace, and men and women of other faiths are given divine power to help others. The only difference is that you and I have made sacred covenants to assist others in partaking the Savior's glorious fruit. And these "divine covenants make strong Christians."[3]

But just because we made covenants at baptism to become the Savior's disciples, we can respond to His invitation to help others with varying degrees of commitment. No one can force us to accomplish our specific mission on earth; and certainly we can go through the motions and never become truly yoked to the Savior. Becoming a serious disciple is a serious matter, one that takes significant effort and commitment. Serious disciples don't boast in their own strength or wisdom (see Alma 26:11–16), for they fully realize they will forfeit the Savior's joy by seeking the praise or glory of others. Serious disciples value their relationships with Heavenly Father and Jesus Christ, and not only rejoice in coming unto Christ personally, but also in knowing "that perhaps [they] may be an be an instrument in the hands of God to bring some soul to repentance" and receive the promised joys of the grand work of salvation (Alma 29:9).

Divine Tools for Human Hands

President Thomas S. Monson said that "we are surrounded by those in need of our attention, our encouragement, our support, our comfort, our kindness—be they family members, friends, acquaintances, or strangers." As the Savior's disciples, "we are the Lord's hands here upon the earth, with the mandate to serve and to lift His children. He is dependent upon each of us."[4]

President Monson likewise promised that "when we are on the Lord's errand, we are entitled to the Lord's help."[5] King Benjamin, one of our greatest examples of service to his fellow man, was "kept and preserved by [God's] matchless power, to serve [his people] with all the might, mind and strength" that God had granted him (Mosiah 2:11). As covenant keepers, we are likewise given a "steady supply of gifts and helps"[6] in the work and glory of others' salvation.

God's priesthood power. First of all, through the oath and covenant of the priesthood, worthy men are authorized to act in Christ's name to utilize God's priesthood power. Elder M. Russell Ballard taught that "when men and women go to the temple, they are both endowed with the same power, which is priesthood power. While the authority of the priesthood is directed through priesthood keys, and priesthood keys are held only by worthy men, access to the power and the blessings of the priesthood is available to all of God's children."[7] Thus as men and women strive to "succor the weak, lift up the hands which hang down, and strengthen the feeble knees," both are rewarded with the joys of ministering angels, the ordinances of salvation, the companionship of the Holy Ghost, and the spirit of prophecy and revelation (D&C 81:5; see also D&C 13, 84).

The organization of the Church of Jesus Christ of Latter-day Saints. Through the Melchizedek Priesthood, we are also blessed with many opportunities to grow in faith through the organization of Christ's Church. In church buildings and temples across the globe, we learn "divine doctrine" and "experience its application" through our associations with one another, and we participate in the ordinances of salvation and help provide them to the living and the dead.[8]

"An endowment of faith." Adding to the gifts of the priesthood and the Church organization, we are blessed by covenants. Making and keeping covenants first "produce the faith necessary to persevere and to do all things that are expedient in the Lord. Our willingness to take upon us the name of Christ and keep His commandments requires a degree of faith, but as we honor our covenants, that faith expands," and then we are granted not only "the promised fruits of obedience," but "the Spirit communicates God's pleasure, and we feel secure in His continued blessing and help."[9]

The gifts of the Spirit. To build the kingdom of God, we likewise receive gifts of the Spirit "for the benefit of the children of God" so "that all may be profited thereby" (D&C 46:26, 12). Some gifts are knowledge, wisdom, healings, faith to work miracles, tongues, interpretation of tongues, prophecy, revelation, and visions (see D&C 46:13–25). Patriarchal blessings help us understand the gifts God has reserved for us, yet we can pray for specific spiritual blessings to help us in our weaknesses. For example, George Q. Cannon said we should pray for the gift of discernment, for it "is of exceeding value and one that should be enjoyed by every Latter-day Saint."[10]

The power of godliness. Adding to these gifts is the power of godliness (D&C 84:20), which, as noted earlier, is gained through temple ordinances and covenant keeping. As we return to the temple and participate in sacred ordinances, we must be "prepared to accept the additional responsibility that comes with added light and spiritual power," and as we honor these covenants, we receive moral and spiritual strength from the grace of God and through the Holy Spirit. The power of godliness strengthens us against the adversary, gives us "the power to smile through hardships,"[11] allows us to help others understand the love of God and His

Son, and enables us to "speak with the tongue of angels" (2 Nephi 31:13; see also 2 Nephi 32:2–3).

Individual talents and abilities. Lastly, because Heavenly Father is a God of creation, He gives us talents that we may know the joys of creating—or "bringing into existence something that did not exist before."[12] A friend of ours is very musically gifted and enjoys creating beautiful and inspiring compositions to lift and inspire others. When I asked him about the joy he feels in bringing others unto Christ through music, he answered with a scripture: "Blessed art thou; for because ye have been diligent in laboring with me in my vineyard, and have kept my commandments, and have brought unto me again the natural fruit, . . . behold ye shall have joy with me because of the fruit of my vineyard" (Jacob 5:75). Our friend concluded that there is joy in knowing our service is accepted of God, but it is greatly magnified when He gives us glimpses into its effect toward the salvation of beloved souls.

With these divine tools, we add our efforts to fulfil the four covenant responsibilities of the Church: "helping members live the gospel of Jesus Christ, gathering Israel through missionary work, caring for the poor and needy, and enabling the salvation of the dead by building temples and performing vicarious ordinances." With each of these duties, we establish relationships with others in order accomplish the Church's overall "purpose [of helping] individuals and families qualify for exaltation."[13] Though these duties are unique in scope, each carries a similar form of joy.

The Joys of Establishing Zion and the Pure in Heart

Let's first look at the joys of helping members of the Church live the gospel of Jesus Christ. We sometimes refer to these labors as "establishing Zion." In our day, Zion is more of a "condition of the heart" than a specific location, but establishing Zion also denotes building up the Lord's Kingdom upon the earth.[14] As members of the Church, "we are part of a covenant people, a community of Saints who encourage, sustain, and minister to one another."[15] United by our individual covenants, we learn from each other how the Savior and His Father love us, and we are taught how to use divine gifts and talents to share that love and to help others keep their covenants to God. We therefore become pure in heart—individually and collectively—through our interactions and relationships with each another.

As we know, service to others in the Church occurs most often through short-term stewardships or callings to act in name of the Lord. I have been greatly blessed through the associations and service of many Saints from past and current wards and stakes, and I likewise feel it a privilege to participate in their salvation! To me, these members are some of the most inspiring and endearing individuals I have ever met. Their lives are shining examples of keeping their baptismal covenants "to bear one another's burdens, that they may be light; . . . to mourn with those that mourn; yea, and comfort those that stand in need of comfort, and to stand as witnesses of God at all times and in all things, and in all places" (Mosiah 18:8–9). Here are a few samples:

- Members sacrifice to set up chairs, make food for luncheons, and attend funerals; but they also sit by those who come to meetings alone, take notes and flowers to those who are afflicted, and extend a listening ear to show genuine concern for others' suffering.
- One sister in my ward makes it a point to sit close to the chapel's pulpit each Sunday so she can show appreciation to the speakers after they give talks.
- One woman visited or called her next-door neighbor every day for a full year after the woman's adult daughter passed away. This grieving mother received an outpouring of love, knowing someone always remembered her sorrow and would help carry her burden.
- One sister refused to take a break from her covenants while in midst of painful chemotherapy treatments. Despite her precarious situation and a germ-filled season, she taught her Relief Society lessons and completed her visiting teaching assignment by mailing her testimony to several women each month.
- Another woman spent hours creating learning journals for the members of her Primary class. Each week, she created a page related to the lesson and placed it in a journal to help the children

remember it and then share it with their families. She also asked others to dress as Nephites or pioneers and even brought artificial trees to create a wonderful Sacred Grove experience for the children.

- In teaching the young women about the Church's covenant obligations, our former stake young women president spent the entire annual budget on supplies for the poor and needy. She wanted these young Saints to rejoice in the divine commission to "succor those that stand in need of your succor" and to "administer of your substance unto him that standeth in need" (Mosiah 4:16). From that time on, stake members—young and old—have met weekly to sew, pack, paint, and organize humanitarian kits to be sent all over the world.[16]

With these examples and many, many more, we can see that covenant keeping is changing the world "every day as we are kind, show love, and take care of each other."[17] Sacred covenants to be Christlike are kept every time service is rendered; every time a prayer is offered on another's behalf; every time lessons are thoughtfully prepared and taught with the Spirit; and every time leaders meet to discuss the needs of the members of their branches, wards, and stakes. As we bring one another to the Savior, we help each other prepare to receive sacred ordinances in the temple and then keep sacred covenants in our respective homes, schools, and communities. And, in this sacred process, all of us are blessed in becoming perfected in Christ.

Obviously, members of the Church of Jesus Christ gain great personal growth through their service, but why does honoring our covenants to bring others unto Christ bring the greatest joys of mortality?

The scriptures teach that "blessed are they who shall seek to bring forth my Zion at that day, for they shall have the gift and the power of the Holy Ghost" (1 Nephi 13:37). With the companionship of the Spirit and the grace of the Son, we are authorized to serve others in Christ's name and with His divine love. We share our love and we share the Lord's love. And that love changes us all. Extending this love generates the joys of strengthened bonds of friendship and fellowship, but, as we become more like Christ, we are allowed to experience the joys felt by Heavenly Father and Jesus Christ when they see our growing progression. Just as "joy shall be in heaven over one sinner that repenteth" (Luke 15:7), we will rejoice that our efforts have helped others in their discipleship to Christ. Heavenly Father allows us to see others through His eyes, and "only then we begin to comprehend the true worth of a soul. . . . Only then can we sense the Savior's caring concern for them," and thereby "be *filled* with 'the pure love of Christ.'"[18]

Oh, what joy we feel knowing that we are able to help others live the gospel of Jesus Christ more fully! We should likewise rejoice knowing that so many people are anxiously engaged and keeping their covenants to bless others—including our lives and the lives of our families! With so many opportunities to serve and be served, the "possibilities" and "elements" of Zion are truly available to us today: "A child's embrace, a companion's caress, a friend's laughter are its materials. Our capacity to mourn another's pain, like God's tears for His children; our desire to lift our neighbor from his destitution, like Christ's desire to lift us from our sin and sorrow—these are not to pass away when the elements shall melt with fervent heat. They are the stuff and substance of any Zion we build, any heaven we inherit."[19]

We Have Great Reason to Rejoice in Proclaiming the Gospel

With the joys of establishing Zion, "children of the covenant" (3 Nephi 20:26) are promised great joy in proclaiming the good news of the gospel to those who are not of our faith. Of missionary work, prophets have declared that "there is no greater joy than bringing souls to Christ. Participation in this great work blesses the convert, blesses the missionary, and blesses those who support the missionary."[20] Others have similarly testified, "What a joyous opportunity. What a remarkable blessing. The Lord, in His kindness, has allowed us to help bring exaltation to His children, our brothers and sisters. Not only, then do we partake of the joy of blessing others, but we become heirs to the blessings of the Abrahamic covenant."[21]

The joys and miracles of missionary service are increasing as the Lord hastens His work of salvation. As compared to my former missionary days, members are more effectively helping the missionaries, and the Lord "is also awakening the minds and opening the hearts of more good and honest people to receive His missionaries."[22] This is in part due to the following inspired changes in missionary work.

- Young men and women are serving as missionaries at younger ages.
- Missionaries are more efficiently studying, training, and teaching the gospel with *Preach My Gospel.*
- Rather than building upon common beliefs, missionaries proclaim our key message: "the Restoration of the gospel of Jesus Christ through the Prophet Joseph Smith."
- Missionaries also emphasize—upfront—that that the reason we are different from other Christian churches is because the Savior's truth, power, and priesthood have been restored and because we hold the Book of Mormon to be "the most correct book on earth, and the keystone of our religion" (Book of Mormon Introduction).
- As opposed to teaching memorized and scripted discussions, missionaries "teach the Savior's message in their own words as guided by the Spirit."
- Instead of using the former "commitment pattern" as a missionary tool, missionaries "focus more on the spiritual conversion an investigator should experience leading up to and through baptism" and temple ordinances.[23]

When our daughter served as a missionary in South America, we were able to appreciate the excitement associated with these new changes. When her progressing investigator Adrian attended church for the first time, he whispered to her, "I didn't hear God." Because he hadn't put forth much effort to feel anything, the sisters prayed before their next visit to see if Adrian was willing to make any further commitments. Surprisingly, Adrian told them he had been thinking a lot about following Christ and wanted to be baptized. He then studied and prayed and faithfully attended church. Following Adrian's baptism, our daughter reported: "The Spirit was overwhelming. I was filled with the Spirit and I just couldn't stop smiling. Adrian has an understanding of the gospel that is absolutely incredible. He understands the scriptures and he loves them." On the following day when Adrian was confirmed a member, she said: "I watched as this shy man humbly partook of the bread and water, and I was filled with joy. I watched as all the branch members congratulated him and as he smiled. There was a confidence about him that wasn't there before. He's finally opened the door, and he understands that he's committed to stay on the path until the end."

The happiness of our daughter and her companion continued as Adrian progressed in the gospel. One week, he was ordained to the priesthood. Another day, he testified of truth after the sisters taught his mother and niece. During "the most spiritual fast and testimony meeting of [her] mission," our daughter rejoiced as Adrian passed the sacrament. Then before she was transferred, Adrian participated in temple ordinances for the first time: "You could see the light and excitement in Adrian's face. Because he was able to be baptized for his father, it was a meaningful experience. Adrian is living the gospel and it shows!!! It has been so wonderful to literally see the change in Adrian's countenance from living the gospel of Jesus Christ. It's evidence to me of the truthfulness of it!"

We hear stories like this all the time, but perhaps we wonder how proclaiming the gospel can create such joy. In addition to the above joys of sharing the Savior's love and feeling the Savior's joy, I testify that missionaries rejoice knowing that God entrusts them to act in His Son's name. But they also have "rejoicings in the joy of [their] brethren" (Alma 30:34) because they more clearly recognize the Lord's hand in their own lives and they personally experience spiritual transformation while witnessing the spiritual rebirth of their investigators.

Think of Alma and the sons of Mosiah. They had been the vilest of sinners, yet after they repented, they never forgot that the Lord had delivered them from such an unrighteous state. Remembering this redemption renewed their joy again and again, and it motivated them to bring others to this same rejoicing. This is why they asked, "Now was not this exceeding joy? Behold, this is joy which none receiveth save it be the truly penitent and humble seeker of happiness" (Alma 27:18). The entire chapter of Alma 26 describes Ammon's rejoicings in experiencing phenomenal missionary success with his companions, and Alma 29 explains Alma's rejoicing in "that which the Lord hath commanded me" to cry repentance to the people. So "great [was Alma's] joy" in the success of his friends that his "soul [was] carried away, even to the separation of it from the body" (Alma 29:9, 16). No wonder these missionaries' many years of bringing others unto Christ were described as "their sufferings in the land, their sorrows, and their afflictions, and their incomprehensible joy" (Alma 28:8).

Glad Tidings of Great Joy in Redeeming the Dead

Now, while it's easy to equate bringing other mortals unto Christ with joy, we may wonder about the joy of bringing the gospel to those who have passed to the other side of the veil—especially when we usually don't see them face-to-face. President Wilford Woodruff said that "there will be very few, if any [of our ancestors], who will not accept the Gospel."[24] Certainly this is a joyous work. When the Prophet Joseph spoke of the glorious possibilities of redeeming our dead, he rejoiced, saying, "Now, what do we hear in the gospel which we have received? A voice of gladness! A voice of mercy from heaven; and a voice of truth out of the earth; glad tidings for the dead; a voice of gladness for the living and the dead; glad tidings of great joy" (D&C 128:19).

Because both my grandmothers had spent their lives in family history research, I was surprised when my first serious experience with "the spirit of Elijah" produced real joy in learning about my great-grandfather's first cousin. Kitty was born in Ireland in 1850, the height of the Irish potato famine, a plague-like period of mass starvation, disease, and emigration from the country. Amazingly, Kitty survived four decades of some of the most destitute years in the Emerald Isle. In 1889, she and her husband were lured into an emigrant scheme by those who had "lied through their teeth and told the desperate Irish they would have houses to live in, seed to sow, machinery to work with, and the most fertile land in the world to farm" in Argentina.[25]

With their seven young children, Kitty and her husband unknowingly boarded the "City of Dresden" Steamship packed with 1,700 other immigrants. After 19 miserable days at sea, the group arrived at their new home undernourished and dehydrated. But worse yet, all the promises of housing, food, seed for planting, and occupational opportunities simply didn't exist. The immigrants were forced to sleep on the ground or were sent to outlying areas, and many died during this period. A census record six years later verified that Kitty and her husband still lived near the docks of Buenos Aires; but, tragically, none of her children were listed with them. Though some of them may have been sent to orphanages, I was heartsick to realize that Kitty had possibly lost several of her children to starvation and disease within a short time of their arrival.

Not long after we learned of Kitty's misfortune, our children performed the proxy baptisms for her family; and soon after that, I was back in the temple participating in other ordinance work for her. At the time, I sensed a bit of her great sufferings and felt an urgent spiritual plea to finish her family's work. Kitty wanted to be sealed to her children and husband for eternity. The day of this sealing ordinance was a memorable and beautiful day. The joy I felt was similar to bringing an investigator unto Christ. I was humbled to have been an instrument to act in the Savior's name, and I was deeply grateful that one of my kindred dead had become a kindred spirit to me. From my experience with Kitty, I learned that the joys of family history research come all along the way. Discovering treasures or jewels about our ancestors' history is exciting and leads to the joys of connecting them to one another through saving ordinances in the temple.

We must not ever lose the glorious and joyous vision of the marvelous work and wonder of the gospel. As the Lord hastens His work in these latter days, we are privileged to act in the name of Christ to help fulfill God's new and everlasting covenant, which is simply the fulness of the gospel of Jesus Christ (see D&C 66:2). With the Savior, the "messenger of the covenant" (3 Nephi 24:1), we offer our time and efforts to bless God's children and "to sustain the Kingdom of God and no other kingdom."[26]

As with life, serious discipleship "is like an old-time rail journey—delays, sidetracks, smoke, dust, cinders and jolts, interspersed only occasionally by beautiful vistas and thrilling bursts of speed. The trick is to thank the Lord for letting you have the ride."[27] Truly, discipleship requires humility, grit, and hard work. It is often inconvenient and sometimes even uncomfortable. But we must remember that "whosoever will lose his life for my sake, the same shall save it" (Luke 9:24) and that "a religion that does not require the sacrifice of all things never has power sufficient to produce the faith necessary unto life and salvation. . . . It [is] through this sacrifice, and this only, that God has ordained that men should enjoy eternal life."[28] Truly, no other adventure in life can compare with the Savior's sweet joys of discipleship—becoming like Him and witnessing the miraculous transformation of others. And we don't want to miss it for the world!

Notes

1. John A. Widtsoe, "The Worth of Souls," *Utah Genealogical and Historical Magazine* (October 1934): 189; as quoted in Carol F. McConkie, "Here to Serve a Righteous Cause," *Ensign,* November 2015.
2. D. Todd Christofferson, "The Power of Covenants," *Ensign,* May 2009.
3. Ibid.
4. Thomas S. Monson, "What Have I Done for Someone Today?" *Ensign,* November 2009.
5. Thomas S. Monson, "To Learn, to Do, to Be," *Ensign,* November 2008.
6. Christofferson, "The Power of Covenants."
7. M. Russell Ballard, "Men and Women in the Work of the Lord," *Ensign,* April 2014.
8. D. Todd Christofferson, "Why the Church?" *Ensign,* November 2015.
9. Christofferson, "The Power of Covenants."
10. George Q. Cannon, as quoted in Robert D. Hales, "Gifts of the Spirit," *Ensign,* February 2002.
11. Christofferson, "The Power of Covenants."
12. Dieter F. Uchtdorf, "Happiness, Your Heritage," *Ensign,* November 2008.
13. Dallin H. Oaks, "Overview of the New Handbooks," *2010 Worldwide Leadership Training Meeting,* November 2010.
14. See "Zion—The Pure in Heart," *Doctrine and Covenants and Church History Gospel Doctrine Teacher's Manual.*
15. Christofferson, "The Power of Covenants." President Spencer W. Kimball also said, "God does notice us, and he watches over us. But it is usually through another person that he meets our needs. Therefore, it is vital that we serve each other in the kingdom. The people of the Church need each other's strength, support, and leadership in a community of believers as an enclave of disciples." ("Selfless Service," in *Teachings of Presidents of the Church: Spencer W. Kimball* [2006], 79–88.)
16. See "Humanitarian Aid," in www.ldswomenofgod.com/?p=102; accessed 23 June 2012; see also Laurie Williams Sowby, "Distant members providing relief to storm victims," *Church News* (September 25, 2004).

17. Carole M. Stephens, "We Have Great Reason to Rejoice," *Ensign,* November 2013.
18. Dale G. Renlund, "Through God's Eyes," *Ensign,* November 2015; emphasis added.
19. Terryl Givens and Fiona Givens, *The God Who Weeps: How Mormonism Makes Sense of Life* (Salt Lake City: Ensign Peak, 2012), 121.
20. Ezra Taft Benson, "A Sacred Responsibility," *Ensign,* May 1986.
21. See "A blessed people," *Church News* (June 28, 2008), 16; see also Abraham 2:9–11.
22. Neil L. Andersen, "It's a Miracle," *Ensign,* May 2013.
23. Benjamin Hyrum White said a draft of *Preach My Gospel,* an "all-inclusive missionary manual," was read by all the members of the First Presidency and the Quorum of the Twelve Apostles, "a testament to the importance of missionary work and the need to have the best materials possible in the hands of missionaries." ("The History of Preach My Gospel," in *Religious Educator* 14, no. 1 (2013): 129–58.
24. Wilford Woodruff, *Millennial Star* (May 28, 1894): 339–40.
25. See www.irlandeses.org/dresden.htm; accessed 16 February 2012.
26. John A. Widtsoe, compiler, *Discourses of Brigham Young* (Salt Lake City: Deseret Book, 1954), 160. As quoted in Russell M. Nelson, "Children of the Covenant," *Ensign,* May 1995.
27. Jenkins Lloyd Jones, "Big Rock Candy Mountains," *Deseret News* (12 June 1973): A4, as quoted in Gordon B. Hinckley, "A Conversation with Single Adults," *Ensign,* March 1997.
28. N. B. Lundwall, comp., *A Compilation Containing the Lectures on Faith* (Salt Lake City: Bookcraft, n.d.), 58; as quoted in Dallin H. Oaks, "Sacrifice," *Ensign,* May 2012.

6: Joy and Rejoicing in Our Posterity

Through the divine plan of salvation, we entered this world into families—the ideal setting for establishing our deepest impressions of joy. God commanded Adam and Eve to multiply and replenish the earth that they might have joy and rejoicing in their posterity (see Genesis 1:28). Like them, we learn that just as we can experience the Savior's joy by coming unto Him, some of the sweetest joys of life are also available as we sacrifice to help our children partake of the fruit of His Atonement. President Gordon B. Hinckley declared that "of all the joys of life, none other equals that of happy parenthood. Of all the responsibilities with which we struggle, none other is so serious. To rear children in an atmosphere of love, security, and faith is the most rewarding of all challenges. The good result from such effort becomes life's most satisfying compensation."[1]

My life has forever been blessed by parents who sacrificed to bring 12 children into the world. Because my siblings and I were never "cheaper by the dozen," my dad worked several jobs to make ends meet, and my mother cooked every meal from scratch—baking ten delicious loaves of bread every other day and multiplying recipes by 20 to accommodate our tribe. Dad taught us to milk cows, drive a tractor, and haul hay; and he even built a greenhouse to teach us the value of work. My mother gave piano lessons to each of us and shared her love of family history and photography. In all my days, I have never heard either of them complain about their many years of sacrificing for their children. Giving of themselves to raise a large family was simply part of life, part of keeping the covenants they made at their temple sealing.

While we have talked about sacrifice with short-term stewardships, nothing can compare to the sacrifices required in permanent stewardships, especially those offered by parents. Over decades of time, mothers and fathers are required to give countless hours of themselves to their offspring. An expectant mother experiences the sacrifices of morning sickness, physical discomfort, and childbirth just to get her child to earth. Then midnight feedings take over her precious sleep and diaper changes and playtime take over her free time. But to offset these great offerings, she will be pleasantly surprised by the sweet joys of a newborn. Her helpless baby who demands her all will nevertheless have the capacity to melt her heart and help her discover a new meaning of love and life. She may even notice that a little smile from one so pure can make up for all she has given up!

These sacrifices are everlastingly linked to our covenants. Elder D. Todd Christofferson explained that covenant keeping is "primarily something that happens at home in the marriage and in the family," for this is where we employ the gospel truths of rescuing and serving and ministering and where efforts to bring others unto Christ is of eternal importance. Therefore, "we go to the temple to make covenants. We go home to keep the covenants."[2]

Emulating Our Eternal Father in Our Parenting

Whether conscious of it or not, covenant-keeping parents sacrifice for their children by patterning their efforts after the perfect Father. Because we aren't able to simply bestow upon our children the type of trust in God that produces lasting conviction and sustaining joy, we sacrifice to love them as Heavenly Father loves us and to teach them as He teaches us.

We start by creating a Garden of Eden-like sanctuary in our homes. This environment is a fortification against the ongoing warfare and addictions of the adversary, but it also operates as a laboratory, a safe place for our children to experiment on the word and prepare them for the demands and temptations of their future lone and dreary worlds.

In the security of our homes, we first sacrifice to establish relationships of trust with our children. We strive to be consistent and trustworthy in our actions—even if we can't trust our children at all times. Like God, we try to provide our children unconditional concern, loyalty, and love; understanding of their hearts and developmental needs; spiritual guidance and instruction; correction in times of need; encouragement and reassurance for making good decisions; a means for repentance and forgiveness; and customized opportunities to complete their goals. And in return, we expect respect, honor, and obedience from our children.

While fostering a sweet and loving relationship with our children, we also sacrifice to teach them to be responsible to us. God teaches responsibility with limits, commandments, and opportunities to learn discipline. And we try to establish a system of rules and expectations for our children's behavior, as well as many experiences for them to practice self-control, self-reliance, honesty, courage, and discipline. We are respectful of their agency, but strive to teach them early—when the price tag of their consequences is small—how to make good choices and to learn to think and act for themselves, rather than to be acted upon by others.

At the same time, we also try to help our children gain an enduring relationship with Heavenly Father and to become responsible to Him and His Son. We lead and guide them in their choices to obey the commandments and repent, to offer their best efforts to God's kingdom, and to submit to His will. As we deliberately teach and testify to them of the Savior's prescribed pathway to joy, we have great hopes that what we do in the home will, in large measure, influence whether our children will continue in divine relationships once they move away from home. Indeed, what we do in our Garden of Eden will determine whether our children teach their own children to find and keep the Savior's joys!

Now, as we model our parenting after our Heavenly Father, we soon realize that we are less than perfect in balancing our efforts to create relationships of trust and to teach responsibility. Like the Taoist Ying Yang, we discover that relationships and responsibilities are each a complementary part of parenting. The only time problems occur is when one is overused at the expense of the other.

For instance, a friend grew up in a home where her parents overemphasized responsibility at the expense of relationships. When she was young, this woman's parents made many of her decisions and used shame as a manipulation to maintain control, causing her to feel insecure and vulnerable to peer pressure. As an adolescent, she felt she could never reach her parents' high expectations—even though she was very bright and talented. Even into adulthood, this friend still could hear the demeaning tone of her parents' "constructive criticism," and became a lifetime people pleaser—even while fighting to repeat this same environment in her own home.

The spiritual damage resulting from this type of imbalance occurs while children are learning trust. When parents feel frustrated that they have "lost control," they withdraw their love and communicate that behaviors are tied to affection and acceptance and that results are more important than progress. Without realizing it, children can likewise feel that God can't love them unconditionally or that their faults and transgressions are too heavy to be forgiven. Other children in this situation may also believe that spiritual development comes by manipulating its timing based solely on their actions (such as setting and reaching goals), perhaps confusing a lack of speed for direction, distance, and joy in the journey. These children may also mistakenly think that the values they can control—such as, honesty, fidelity, and chastity—are more important than those they develop with others—such as mercy, love, unselfishness, kindness, and sensitivity.

As devastating as it is to focus on responsibility over relationships, we are apt to wonder what happens when relationships are emphasized at the expense of responsibility. The answer is that establishing *quality* relationships *never* creates problems for children. In fact, looking to our perfect Father, we can see that parenting with an overabundance of love and care only makes things better for both the parent and the child!

Problems with relationship-based parenting only arise when parents confuse how relationships are truly developed in the first place. Some parents avoid teaching responsibility all in the name of relationship building. Hoping to win their children's affection with few rules and insufficient expectations, parents become too permissive, "afraid to counsel with [their children] for fear of offending them"[3] and apt to encourage irresponsible children whose sense of entitlement is coupled with a lack of initiative. Other parents avoid teaching responsibility simply because they want to rescue children from completing difficult tasks or making difficult decisions—all of which demonstrate a lack of parental confidence and offer little preparation for the child's future.

Incorrect assumptions of how relationships are established further skew a child's spiritual understanding of what is required of a disciple of Christ. Without the teachings of responsibility, children may grow up assuming that faith and miracles have little to do with work, or that becoming Christlike in meekness, long-suffering, and charity doesn't require disciplined time and prayerful effort. Parents who don't understand the true meaning of relationship building may even downplay the consequences of their children's transgressions, possibly insulating them from the full price of repentance—and also the Savior's joys of forgiveness. When this happens, the underlying message is that His Atonement doesn't have the power to cleanse them of their sins, to strengthen them in their adversity, or to heal them from spiritual pain.

From these examples, we can see why balancing healthy relationships and establishing age-appropriate responsibilities is critical to our parenting—and to our discovering and retaining the Savior's joys. I learned more about this balancing act when my young son, Michael, lost yet another important item he needed for school. As it was my tendency to overemphasize responsibility over relationships, I prepared to give him an extra lecture about being more careful with his things. But the Spirit whispered that this was only part of his development and that he also needed to see the workings of God in his life. With heaven's grace, I purged myself of disappointment and told Michael that Heavenly Father knew everything about everything and could help us find what he needed if we but asked in prayer. I then privately poured my heart out to God, asking that Michael would gain a testimony of His love through personal prayer.

Throughout the next week, both Michael and I searched high and low, and I continued to carry a prayer in my heart that his prayers would be answered. One night, I happened to be with Michael in his room when he opened the top dresser drawer and discovered the lost item buried underneath his clothing. Both of us were relieved, but I was grateful he had been the one to find it. Moments later, I then realized that the only window of time both of us had been together was during the previous few minutes. Finding this object would have satisfied my pleadings, but the Lord had intended for each of us to experience a tender mercy—all at the same time! I testified to Michael that Heavenly Father hears and answers prayers and that the timing of the search was not coincidental. I then received my own joyful witness that God indeed loves His children who are children, and He loves His children who are parents! Overjoyed that Michael had recognized God's hand in his life, I felt empowered to work on building a stronger relationship of trust with my son.

Even when we are imperfect in our parenting, Heavenly Father is the perfect parent to all of us. He perfectly knows our needs, He perfectly knows the needs of our children, and His perfect timing is evidence of His great goodness and love. Through divine revelation, God can help us identify our parental imbalances—strengths and weaknesses stemming from differing family backgrounds—and give us specific ways to modify our parenting methods to become more like His. Then, as we seek further inspiration to understand each of our children's developmental needs, God will teach us how to balance their levels of relationship and responsibility. We will know whether we need to encourage greater diligence in their schoolwork, help them find employment, or create more opportunities for social activities and strengthening friendships.

If we but ask God in faith, we will "receive revelation upon revelation, knowledge upon knowledge, that [we] mayest know the mysteries and peaceable things—that which bringeth joy, that which bringeth life eternal" (D&C 42:61). Truly, God "has entrusted these particular children to [us] and . . . He will help [us] know how to guide each child toward the fulfillment of his or her divine potential."[4]

Following the Savior in Our Sacrifice

As we try to emulate our Eternal Father and to hearken to His Spirit, we also must strive to follow the Savior in our sacrifice to our children. After Adam and Eve were driven from the Garden of Eden, they offered sacrifices unto the Lord without really understanding why. An angel appeared to them and explained that "this thing is a similitude of the sacrifice of the Only Begotten of the Father, which is full of grace and truth" (Moses 5:7 [6–7]). Indeed, everything we give up for the gospel's sake—our tithing and fast offerings; our service in callings, in the temple, or as missionaries; our sustaining of the kingdom of God; and our sacrifice to our children—is in similitude or likeness of the great atoning sacrifice of the Son of God.[5]

As previously discussed, we add our sacrifice to the Savior's great atoning sacrifice to obtain the cleansing, strengthening, and healing powers of His Atonement. We offer to God our willingness to believe that He will magnify our imperfect efforts to nurture our children through the grace of His Son. And we then offer our willingness to bear our children's burdens, to mourn with them when they suffer tragedies and disappointments, to comfort them whenever they are in need, and to stand as a witness of God to them at all times (see Mosiah 18:8–9). All of these bits of sacrifice help lead our children to the Savior, who helps us all back to our Heavenly Father. Then with the grace of the Savior, our sacrifice helps lead our children to the Son of God and back Home.

In 1833, the Prophet Joseph received further revelation from the Lord about our sacrifices. As the Saints were facing severe persecution and necessary sacrifices to leave Jackson County, the Savior said: "Verily I say unto you, all among them who know their hearts are honest, and are broken, and their spirits contrite, and are willing to observe their covenants by sacrifice—yea, every sacrifice which I, the Lord, shall command—they are accepted of me" (D&C 97:8; emphasis added). For the early members of the Church and for all of us, this scripture helps us understand that the Lord knows what we must give up to keep our covenants. He accepts even our smallest sacrifice and assures us that by living according to His will, we can become "a very fruitful tree," a mature and faithful disciple whose "precious fruit" (D&C 97:9) are those we bring with us to Christ.

As we observe our covenants by sacrifice, we can feel confident that both the Eternal and Omniscient Father of our spirits and "the Master of oceans and earth and skies"[6] have all the answers to our most pressing questions. We don't need to rely on our limited knowledge of how to best succor and teach our children. As we seek God's Spirit, we can receive the grace of His Son to be capable of hearkening to the promptings of how and when and what to sacrifice for our children. The reward for our sacrifice is witnessing their incremental spiritual rebirth, precisely why we will "have no greater joy than to hear that [our] children walk in truth" (3 John 1:4; see also D&C 109:15).

My favorite scriptural illustration of those sacrificing by covenant is the fathers and mothers of the stripling warriors. After learning the gospel truths, these parents' hearts were changed through faith in God. The fathers thus buried their weapons of war and over a thousand of them were slaughtered rather than breaking a sacred covenant with God. In the end, the powerful sacrifice of these righteous fathers and mothers—many of them later as single mothers—taught sons and daughters the most powerful lessons of life:

- To give unto their brethren, rather than to take (Alma 24:18)
- To labor abundantly with their hands, rather than spend their days in idleness (Alma 24:18)
- To know the importance of covenant making and keeping (see Alma 53:16, 18)
- To be physically strong and to be active (Alma 53:20)
- To become valiant and courageous (Alma 53:20)
- To be "true at all times in whatsoever thing they were entrusted" (Alma 53:20)
- To become men (and women) of truth and soberness (Alma 53:21)
- To keep the commandments of God and to walk uprightly before Him (Alma 53:21)
- To obey and observe to perform every word of command with exactness (Alma 57:21)
- To not fear death but to have hope in the resurrection and the redemption (Alma 56:47; 27:28)
- To value the liberty of their fathers more than their own lives (Alma 56:47)

- To believe in the existence of a just God and to continually trust Him (Alma 57:26–27)
- To become firm and undaunted—to doubt not that God would preserve them and deliver them by His marvelous power (Alma 57:27)
- To rely upon the words and the testimony of their mothers, for they testified, "We do not doubt our mothers knew it" (Alma 56:48)

Although we always tie the military miracles of the stripling warriors to the sacrifice of their parents, we sometimes forget that we likewise are entitled to miracles as we willingly keep our covenants by sacrifice. When we do as the Lord commands, the windows of heaven open and we are strengthened to give of ourselves in ways we couldn't offer alone. God bestows upon us the divine tools of increased faith, the power of the priesthood, the gifts of the Spirit, the organization of the Church, the power of godliness, and talents and abilities to raise children in love and righteousness. Through the medium of the Spirit and because of Savior's sacrifice, we are empowered to nurture, direct, and forgive our children; our parental weaknesses are transformed into strengths; and our resources and efforts are magnified in ways that promote our children's trust in and obedience to God.

Giving of Ourselves, But Not Giving Up

As the joys of parenthood usually come through honoring our covenants by sacrifice, I must add a final word about perseverance and endurance. Whenever I think of the stresses of parenthood and how often I forget to pace myself, I recall the time I was tempted to run a footrace with my young daughter. She remembers this race because she won, but I remember it because I pulled a muscle in my leg and walked with a limp for days! I later pulled a "spiritual muscle" as a result of feeling overwhelmed with my children and with my calling and promises I felt I needed to keep. In this state of emotional and spiritual exhaustion, I said something unkind to another child, and the following days were filled with godly sorrow for hurting one of God's children. Interestingly, this spiritual injury took much longer to heal compared to the physical one.

Parenthood is comparable to a challenging and refining marathon, "an endurance race filled with obstacles" all along the way.[7] When children are overscheduled and parents are overspent, it is easy to "hit the wall" of fatigue and energy loss, as well as emotional and spiritual depletion. King Benjamin reveals that the secret is learning to avoid running faster than we have strength (see Mosiah 4:27) or as Paul said, "[To] run with patience the race that is set before [you]" (Hebrews 12:1).

Endurance in the race of parenting is especially critical when dealing with a child's poor choices. Just as parents feel great joy when their children walk in faith, we also feel extreme sorrow when one strays from obedience, repentance, remembering, and covenant keeping.

A dedicated mother I know is a faithful woman who spent years exercising her faith in behalf of her wayward son. As she pled again and again for divine help, she eventually discovered gifts that God was waiting for her to open. One was the gift of understanding that her son's exercise of agency was indeed beautiful—oftentimes reckless and dangerous—but beautiful nonetheless. Another gift from God was knowing that her efforts of praying and fasting for her son to act a certain way would only leave her resentful of her sacrifice and that trying to coerce him to live righteously was much less successful than asking how God would have *her* act toward him. In her need for spiritual survival, she increased her relationship with Heavenly Father and her discipleship to the Son. As never before, she knew of God's love for her and her son and recognized she didn't need to mistakenly connect her self-worth with his behavior. Above all, she was strengthened to preserve her relationship with her son and to not give up on him.

Because the blessings of the sealing covenant also flow to their children, parents can be reassured that continued faithfulness to covenants can help bring their wayward children back to Christ. Joseph Fielding Smith taught that "those born under the covenant, throughout all eternity, are the children of their parents. Nothing except the unpardonable sin, or sin unto death, can break this tie. If children do not sin . . . 'unto death,' the parents may still feel after them and eventually bring them back near to them again."[8] Though faithful parents cannot automatically "save disobedient children,"[9] honoring their covenants by sacrifice can help to turn their children's hearts back to Christ—even when they are on the other side of the veil. This is one reason we must never give up on our efforts to offer a broken heart and a contrite spirit to God, and it is the most important reason we must never give up on our children.

Now, if you think you will need to tap into the Savior's enabling powers when your children disappoint you, consider how much you will need it when you find disappointment in your own parenting. Once, during a difficult setback of parental failure, my self-confidence became so weak that I felt paralyzed to act in faith. Knowing what was expected of me, I was overcome with a heavy burden of guilt. As much as I tried to shake this feeling, the adversary kept showing me the stark difference between the ideal and the individual and between revelation and reality. Failing God in this way, I wasn't sure I could ever live up to His expectations again.

In desperation, I turned to the scriptures and found comfort from prophets who had recorded their shortcomings and their resulting recommitment to God. In reading about Peter's life, I sensed his terrible grief at the crowing of the cock and wondered what torture he must have felt upon comparing his denial to the betrayal of Judas Iscariot. I realized that his running to the tomb upon Resurrection morning was motivated with a unique need for reconciliation. When studying Nephi's overwhelming challenges as the new prophet, I wondered how he transitioned from "O wretched man that I am!" to "Rejoice, O my heart, and give place no more for the enemy of my soul" (2 Nephi 4:17, 28). The more I pondered Nephi's situation, the more I felt that Heavenly Father recognized Nephi's willingness to believe and willingness to do, and somehow, some way, God reassured His servant of His divine confidence.

In a moment of great surprise, I then discovered that throughout my intense period of self-doubt, I had received numerous flashes of edification, revelation, and promptings from the Spirit, some of which had blessed others with pivotal answers to overwhelming challenges. Even while doubting my abilities, Heavenly Father had yet trusted me with His Spirit and had continued to allow me to act in the name of His Son. Surely, this was evidence of God's love for me. But it was also proof of His confidence in my ability to be trustworthy. And if He had confidence in me, I could have confidence that He would help me to fulfill covenants in behalf of my family members.

I testify that Heavenly Father is truly counting on us to make a difference in the lives of our children! For this reason, we must never give up on ourselves, our children, or God! When the journey seems long, we must "not slacken [our] strength because of [our] afflictions" (2 Nephi 4:29). And when our hearts are depressed and we are about to retreat, we must continue on and "bear with patience [our] afflictions, and [He] will give unto [us] success" (Alma 26:27). As we combine our sacrifice with the sacrifice of the Savior, we will experience joy and rejoicing in our posterity. Like Adam and Eve, we will more fully understand our blessed privilege to experience mortality, offering a broken heart and a contrite spirit that "in this life [we] shall have joy, and again in the flesh [we] shall see God" (Moses 5:10 [10–12]).

How grateful we must be for the sacrifice of Jesus Christ! Because of Him, the sealing power binds us to one another and enables our family relationships to last forever. Because of Him, we can receive revelation and renewed stores of faith and energy to bring our children unto Him. And because of Him, giving of ourselves to our children will be rewarded with the most priceless joys of parenthood—knowing our children can trust God enough to allow the gospel truths to become etched in their hearts and knowing they can replicate the Savior's joy in the future.

Notes

1. Gordon B. Hinckley, "Save the Children," *Ensign,* November 1994.
2. D. Todd Christofferson, "The Gospel Answers Life's Problems and Challenges" in *Worldwide Leadership Training Meeting*, February 2012.
3. Robert D. Hales, "With All the Feeling of a Tender Parent: A Message of Hope to Families," *Ensign,* May 2004; as quoted in Larry R. Lawrence, "Courageous Parenting," *Ensign,* November 2010.
4. See "Children Are an Heritage of the Lord," in *Marriage and Family Relations Instructor's Manual* (2000), 43–48.
5. Monte J. Brough "Living the Law of Sacrifice," *Ensign,* April 2000.
6. "Master, the Tempest Is Raging," *Hymns,* no. 105.
7. Richard J. Maynes, "The Strength to Endure," *Ensign,* November 2013.
8. Joseph Fielding Smith, *Doctrines of Salvation, Vol. II* (Salt Lake City: Bookcraft, 1955), 90–91. See also James E. Faust, "Dear Are the Sheep That Have Wandered," *Ensign,* May 2003.
9. Smith, *Doctrines of Salvation,* 91.

7: The Crowning *Joys* of Celestial Marriage

Even compared to the joys of motherhood or fatherhood, the relationships in marriage have the potential for achieving the greatest of the Savior's joys. President Spencer W. Kimball said that "marriage can be, more an exultant ecstasy than the human mind can conceive. This is within the reach of every couple, every person."[1]

Many a love song and a romance novel will attest that finding one's true love is an exhilarating and intoxicating experience. Most marriages begin with this kind of joy, and almost all brides and grooms expect to "live happily ever after." Unfortunately, about half of all marriages in Western cultures end in divorce when the "dreams of a happy marriage [are] shattered in the real world of dirty dishes, unpaid bills, conflicting work schedules, and crying babies."[2]

Whenever we think of the stresses affecting marital bliss, we must remember that this world is the telestial world, and "the god of this world hath blinded the minds of them which believe not" (2 Corinthians 4:4). Satan's influence is seen in the decline of societal morals and the rise of sin and violence, but his greatest aim is to destroy marriage and family relationships.[3] He would that all couples remain in a never-ending telestial existence by following the voices of the great and spacious building. He entices some to live together before marriage and others to divorce. But more than ever before, Satan promotes addiction and abuse—his most toxic weapons—to damage relationships by weakening trust in others and by weakening trust in God.

Yet, despite these potential snares, we wisely chose to come to this telestial world to qualify for celestial glory. Here, we are given opportunities to use our agency that our souls "be sanctified from all unrighteousness" and "prepared for the celestial glory; For after [our soul] hath filled the measure of its creation, it shall be crowned with glory, even with the presence of God the Father" (D&C 88:18–19). As members of the Church, our goal "should be to fill the measure of our creation as sons and daughters of our Heavenly Father—that is, to reach exaltation and eternal life."[4] We do so by coming unto Christ and by bringing others with us. In marriage, we bring each other unto the Savior as we receive sacred ordinances, keep covenants to become all that God desires of us, and then together gain God's marvelous promises (see D&C 84:38).

Lessons from a Love Story

Two of my ancestors enjoyed a wonderful marriage together. Their love story helps us understand how couples progress in a telestial world and qualify together for celestial glory. Annie and John were born in neighboring Utah towns and became high school sweethearts. Just before the Depression, John graduated from college and moved to New York City to continue his studies. After a year of being apart, Annie received his marriage proposal in the mail, which invited her to become his "chief cook and bottle washer." She accepted the offer, stipulating a temple marriage as part of the deal. John had not participated in Church activity in his youth, but he had attended his Manhattan branch and was worthy of this blessing. After their sealing in the Salt Lake Temple, the newlyweds became reacquainted while traveling back east by train, and then honeymooned—as they called it—for the next four years in New York.

When they moved home, John took over his father's construction business and Annie took care of the children while he worked all week away from home. For the next two decades, she was the primary caretaker of their four children and used common sense and the Savior's teachings to shape their habits and beliefs. Though often apart, John and Annie's relationship continued to deepen. John adored Annie and respected her loyalty to the children and to the Church, and he encouraged her to develop her talents and community friendships. Annie also cherished him by supporting his growing business and by praising his good qualities. Of him she claimed that no father was prouder of his kids and no family could boast of more happiness.

Though John did not actively participate within the Church, he and Annie nevertheless experienced happiness in their family and married life. By applying the principles of Jesus Christ in their relationship with one another, they truly enjoyed marital unity and purpose, affection and appreciation, emotional support and encouragement, and security and commitment.

After they had been married for 22 years, John experienced a mighty change of heart at the funeral of one of his work associates. The man had taken a trip to visit relatives and there had realized the limitation of his material wealth. Resolving to devote more of his time to the things that mattered, he started for home. Unfortunately, only a few hours later, his car went out of control, and he died before he could make good on his promises. John was deeply affected by this man's death and began consciously changing his life. He gave up his coffee, worked to deepen his relationships with his wife and children, and began to attend church meetings. His renewed activity meant altering his former attitude of being willing to do anything for the Church except preach or pray. When asked to give a prayer, he wrote one down so he could read it later. When he was asked to speak in church, Annie wrote his "two and a half minute" talks and he delivered them verbatim at the pulpit. And when he accepted a calling to serve as the Elder's Quorum President, he began practicing what he taught—praying at home.

As Annie consecrated her heart to support his spiritual growth, John began to recognize God's goodness in his life. John began to understand that neither he, nor Annie, could become all that God desired without divine help. As John then sought to attain a deeper faith, his weaknesses transformed into strengths and he felt more confidence sharing spiritual counsel with others. Little by little, John embraced the joys Annie had already known about serious discipleship to Christ. They each tried to honor baptismal covenants to love others and to be a witness of God at all times. Not only did they serve faithfully in their callings to help other members live the gospel of Jesus Christ more fully, but they also rejoiced in their children's missionary successes, and participated in redeeming the dead and caring for those in need. And the best indicator of their increasing joy of following Christ was their deepening love for one another.

Years later, John was called to serve as a bishop and gradually learned to juggle all his family, church, business, and community obligations. But then without warning—and through no fault of his own—his business suddenly crumbled. John, a successful and seasoned contractor, realized that decades of growth had vanished overnight and that their sole source of financial stability had disappeared with it. Both he and Annie were devastated by the loss. Each became physically ill and couldn't take pleasure in simple joys. It was difficult to stay cheerful or even keep up a conversation together.

Submitting to this divine tutorial, John and Annie sought personal revelation and relied on the Savior's grace to stay true to their sealing covenant—to God and to each other. They became afflicted in one another's afflictions, meaning his challenges became hers and vice versa. Their faithfulness was rewarded with backs strong enough to carry their heavy burden and reassurance that Heavenly Father would turn their affliction to their gain. John was further enabled to avoid bankruptcy by liquidating the company assets for a small salary, and then spent the next three grueling years painting and selling almost every piece of equipment to pay off his creditors and the bank. John and Annie recognized these as miracles from the Lord.

In gratitude for this sustaining power, John and Annie renewed their efforts to God's great work. They not only employed their resources and talents for increasingly worthwhile projects, but many of their most significant contributions were made during this season of growth. The recipients were ward and stake members, their community, their kindred dead, and especially their children and grandchildren—they who knew very little of their overwhelming challenges. Annie and John often gathered their posterity together and let them know they were a big reason for their joy. At one of John's last Thanksgiving holidays with his family, he quietly watched the chaos of his children and grandchildren interacting and openly wept tears of gratitude and joy.

By the time John's health began to deteriorate, both he and Annie had become more like the Savior, and their afflictions were "swallowed up in the joy of Christ" (Alma 31:38). During these difficult days, they were seldom apart. Annie drove John to doctor appointments and moved her projects near his chair at home. And when Annie experienced her own physical problems, she gratefully wrote of his devotion, saying that his kindness, consideration, and supportiveness had always been her best strength and that he had always been her best fan. When John passed away, his family all mourned his loss, yet Annie experienced the deep sorrow of lingering in mortality without her beloved companion. She continued to bless the lives of others, faithfully enduring her mortal probation until the day of her joyful reunion with her sweetheart.

While John and Annie's story is certainly one of deep love for each other, it is also a story of God's love for them. As they consecrated themselves to one another and to His Son, He also consecrated their performance for their gain and purified their hearts. Over time, Heavenly Father filled their souls with joy and consolation, and they grew to love one another, "even as Christ also loved the church, and gave himself for it" (Ephesians 5:25). And I am confident that the joys they found on earth have continued in the spirit world and that in a future day they will be "swallowed up in a fulness of joy"[5] and exalted glory.

From Telestial to Terrestrial—Happiness Founded upon Jesus Christ

To understand how we can likewise progress to celestial vistas in our marriages and then ultimately gain the promises of eternal life and exaltation with our spouses, we must first recognize the difference between telestial and terrestrial marriages. Those who inherit the telestial kingdom are those who "live after the manner of the world"[6] and who "received not the gospel of Christ, neither the testimony of Jesus" (D&C 76:82 [81]). These are men and women who have been persuaded by Satan "to do evil, and believe not in Christ, and deny him, and serve not God" (Moroni 7:17). On the other hand, those who inherit terrestrial glory are honorable men and women "who were blinded by the craftiness of men" and members of the Church who were "not valiant in the testimony of Jesus." They will "receive of the presence of the Son, but not of the fulness of the Father" (D&C 76:75, 79, 77).

In the story we have considered, we can see that John was an honorable man but not valiant in keeping his covenants. In this terrestrial state, he yet felt undeniable happiness when following principles of the Savior. This was possible because "every thing which inviteth and enticeth to do good, and to love God, and to serve him, is inspired of God" (Moroni 7:13, 19). Truly, "happiness in family life is most likely to be achieved when founded upon the teachings of the Lord Jesus Christ. Successful marriages and families are established and maintained on principles of faith, prayer, repentance, forgiveness, respect, love, compassion, work, and wholesome recreational activities."[7]

Now, while her husband was still living a terrestrial life, Annie was earnestly trying to honor the covenants she had made in the temple. I am sure this situation was challenging because Satan knows he can inflict damage to a marriage when one spouse wholly strives to keep promises to God and the other does not. One faithful woman explained to me once that the day her husband said he wasn't going to church again was the saddest day of her life (and the beginning of the end of their marriage). Another friend tearfully explained that she had received revelation in the temple to resolve marital difficulties; but because her husband had lost trust in God, he wouldn't accept her inspiration, nor would he ask for divine help himself. Still another friend sensed her husband's insecurities whenever she discussed her newfound gospel insights. He couldn't understand her excitement for this kind of revelation; and though unintentional on her part, he felt patronized and manipulated whenever she brought up her spiritual progression.

Realizing how overwhelmingly sorrowful this kind of a marriage is and can be, we must teach our youth to follow the prophetic counsel of President Gordon B. Hinckley: "Marry the right person in the right place at the right time. . . . Choose a companion you can always honor, you can always respect, one who will complement you in your own life, one to whom you can give your entire heart, your entire love, your entire allegiance, your entire loyalty."[8] But, at the same time, none of us should lose hope for those who are struggling in their marriages—especially for those in temple marriages. Heavenly Father knows and loves each of His children and wants to bless and inspire them in their marriage relationships. Couples can improve their relationships simply by remembering to draw near to Him and to qualify for His Spirit and the power of the Savior's Atonement. Elder Jeffrey R. Holland declared, "However late you think you are, however many chances you think you have missed, however many mistakes you feel you have made or talents you think you don't have, or however far from home and family and God you feel you have traveled, I testify that you have *not* traveled beyond the reach of divine love."[9]

Those waiting for a spouse to come unto Christ can also feel optimistic that God will provide divine tools and talents to enhance marital relationships, as well as the enabling power of His Son to act upon divine promptings. One friend was given a spiritual impression before accepting a proposal from a worthy young man that they would need marital counseling someday. She agreed to marry him in the temple and now explains her greatest joy comes when her husband gains line-upon-line knowledge about how to live the gospel and come unto Christ. Even with the help of trained professionals, she understands her spiritual progression comes through her relationship with Heavenly Father and her discipleship with Christ. With heaven's grace, she is given direction to repent and to change herself, and she is given reassurance that even though she can't change her husband, the Savior can.

Because of the Savior's sacrifice, there is great hope that every relationship can improve with His pure love! Truly, there is joy in knowing that His cleansing, strengthening, and healing power can and should be sought as we ask for His help in forgiving, supporting, and succoring one another. And while any improvement in a mortal relationship may not automatically enhance a spouse's relationship to God, it *can* enhance human trust and security—the very elements that can potentially spark spiritual growth and open doors for divine relationships.

From Terrestrial to Celestial—the Power of Covenant Keeping

Recognizing that the potential for change, growth, and transformation is the principle purpose for the Savior's Atonement, we can understand why we should not settle for a terrestrial existence or a terrestrial marriage. A celestial marriage includes all the rewards of terrestrial marriage, but, as Annie and John learned, its quality "[differs] in glory as the moon differs from the sun" (D&C 76:78). President Russell M. Nelson even proclaimed that "celestial marriage brings greater possibilities for happiness than does any other relationship."[10]

As opposed to those who inherit terrestrial glory, men and women who enter into the celestial kingdom have "received the testimony of

Jesus," were "baptized after the manner of his burial," and "receive the Holy Spirit by the laying on of the hands of him who is ordained and sealed unto this power" (D&C 76:51–52). Elder Joseph Fielding Smith further explained that "baptism is the door into the celestial kingdom" and that "all the ordinances of the gospel pertain to the celestial kingdom."[11] Receiving priesthood ordinances and keeping their associated covenants is thus the difference between a terrestrial marriage and a celestial marriage.

With this revelation, we can conclude that simply keeping our baptismal covenants qualifies us for the celestial kingdom. Knowing this, we wonder how honoring baptismal covenants, as well as the covenants of the endowment, can profoundly affect our marriages and bring the Savior's joy into our relationship. The answer is twofold. As we strive to become Christlike through covenant keeping, the Savior's grace first cleans our hands and purifies our hearts, and then our spouse indirectly and directly benefits from our increased responsibility to God. Indeed, discipleship to the Savior produces His joys of increased patience, integrity, compassion, respect, hope, kindness, and loyalty. And no other mortal will gain more from the development of these attributes than our spouse!

Secondly, keeping our covenants to become Christlike inherently means we will help one another come unto the Savior. Covenant-keeping husbands will encourage their wives to become women of God, those who "know how to make important things happen by their faith," those who use "the gift of discernment" to "view the trends in the world,"[12] and those who have a "reverence for motherhood, even when that blessing has been withheld from them for a time."[13] At the same time, covenant-keeping wives will help their husbands "rise up" and become men of God, those who honor the gift of the priesthood, sustain and defend God's kingdom upon the earth,[14] and those who wax strong in the presence of God with virtuous thoughts and the pursuit of pure knowledge (D&C 121:45). Although a covenant-keeping wife may feel she is more organized and creative and effective at family home evenings, scripture study, and family prayers, she will encourage her husband to become the patriarch of the home—he who is responsible for the spiritual wellbeing of the family[15] and he who counsels with his wife in applying the gospel to the needs of their family.

Covenant keeping in a celestial marriage requires sacrifice. Just before my husband and I knelt at the altar to be married, the temple sealer turned and asked him, "What is the one thing your bride will want most in marriage?" After waiting for an appropriate response, the sealer simply said: "Just you." He then explained to us (and to all our wedding guests) that if a husband sacrifices his attention and time and consideration for his wife, and if a wife sacrifices for him in return, all other things would fall into place in their marriage. Certainly, spending quality and quantity time for one another demonstrates that next to our relationships to the Father and the Son, the marital relationship is the most important—more important than those with parents, siblings, friends, or children. This knowledge provides spouses with a sense of security that can be gained no other way.

Sometimes it takes a miracle to coordinate schedules to go on dates together, attend the temple together, read scriptures together, and even pray together as a couple. But we must not forget that the Father of heaven and earth is a God of miracles. He has a vested interest in our covenant-keeping efforts, and He knows that marriage can and should be a spiritual experience. Because His Spirit helped get couples to the altars of the temple, He wants them to do things together that ensure they will always have His Spirit in their relationships. With the Holy Ghost, emotional and spiritual bonds between man and wife increase, building reservoirs of trust and fidelity and rekindling romance in marriage. God will send His Spirit so both spouses know how to sacrifice for one another, and He will send reassurances that He approves of their efforts.

Onto Exaltation—Aligning Our Wills and Offering Our Souls

Just as baptism is the door for entering the celestial realm, "celestial marriage is the gate to exaltation."[16] From Joseph Smith, "we learn that there are three degrees within the celestial kingdom. To be exalted in the highest degree and continue eternally in family relationships, we must enter into 'the new and everlasting covenant of marriage' and be true to that covenant" (D&C 131:1–4).[17] "To be exalted—or to gain exaltation—refers to the highest state of happiness and glory in the celestial realm."[18] Because "temple marriage is a requirement for obtaining the highest degree of celestial glory," "all who are worthy to enter into the new and everlasting covenant of marriage will have that opportunity, whether in this life or the next."[19]

The new and everlasting covenant of marriage, which is also called celestial marriage,[20] is a two-way promise made at sacred temple altars and by the power of the Melchizedek Priesthood. It is the crowning covenant of the new and everlasting covenant (or the gospel of Jesus Christ). Through this sealing ordinance, Heavenly Father makes individual and joint promises to a husband and wife, and they "*individually* and *separately* make promises, commitments, and covenants" to God and then covenant to "receive each other as husband and wife."[21] Because temple ordinances are associated with covenants to live a Christlike life, I believe that an important part of the new and everlasting covenant of marriage is the promise to live a Christlike life *for each other*.

Certainly, disregarding these promises to God and to one another causes a marriage to suffer. Elder Cree-L Kofford said that "whenever there is a difficulty between a husband and wife in their marriage relationship that is serious enough to threaten that relationship, one or the other (or both) is not living the gospel of Jesus Christ."[22] On the other hand, "*celestial marriage* is what [husband and wife] create by being true to the sacred covenants [they] make during the temple marriage ceremony."[23] As married couples strive to keep the sacred promises of the sealing ordinance, they are blessed according to their individual faithfulness and "as one." The reward of exaltation is specifically "conditioned upon [their] joint faithfulness."[24]

While we know little about the Savior's "fulness of joy" in an exalted state, we know that "God's purpose is that we, His children, may be able to experience ultimate joy, to be with Him eternally, and to become even as He is."[25] The Lord compared the glory of the celestial kingdom to that of the sun and He compared the glory of the lowest kingdom to that of the stars (D&C 76:70, 81). And if "the glory of the telestial . . . surpasses all understanding" (D&C 76:89), think of the grand blessings reserved for those who honor the new and everlasting covenant of marriage! Elder Tad R. Callister taught that the more we explore, research, and analyze the influence of the Savior's atoning sacrifice, "the further its boundaries seem to expand, almost with endless elasticity."[26] Because of the Son of God, we can be given incomprehensible rewards in our earthly marriage and exaltation in the life to come. Here is but a brief summary.

Increased knowledge, peace, and hope on earth. Just as Annie and John learned, "if [husband and wife] love God enough and follow His teachings, everything else will work out just fine and [they] will be blessed to find solutions"[27] to their deepest problems. With an outpouring of the Spirit and the power of godliness of the temple, couples will gain spiritual insights and guidance needed to understand how best to work toward a happy and successful marriage. As spouses continue to support the spiritual rebirth of one another, their relationship will ascend to higher and higher levels of peace, satisfaction, and joy, and they will "obtain a sufficient hope" to "enter into the rest of the Lord" (Moroni 7:3). Entering into His rest means husbands and wives will discover deepened faith in God's plan, assurances they are living according to His will, and "rest from religious turmoil," meaning they will not be "disturbed by every wind of doctrine, or by the cunning and craftiness of men who lie in wait to deceive."[28]

Living with God and becoming like Him in the eternities. While celestial glory means "[dwelling] in the presence of God and his Christ forever and ever" (D&C 76:62), exaltation in the highest degree of this kingdom also includes partaking of Their "fulness of joy" (Psalm 16:11) and becoming like Them.[29] No mortal can begin to comprehend what it means to become all that God is and to gain all that He hath (see D&C 84:38). But if both spouses qualify for this fulness of joy, they will be "sealed by the Holy Spirit of promise" (D&C 76:53), a witness of the Holy Ghost "to the Father that the saving ordinances have been performed properly and that the covenants associated with them have been kept."[30] Worthy couples will not only gain glorious and perfected bodies at the first Resurrection, but will also be united eternally and purified in purpose and attribute. Moreover, they "shall receive their inheritance and be made equal with [God]" (D&C 88:107). They [shall be] gods, even the sons of God—wherefore, all things [will be] theirs" (D&C 76:58–59). They "shall pass by the angels, and the gods, which are set there, to their exaltation and glory in all things"; and the glory of their reward "shall be a fulness and a continuation of their seeds forever and ever" (D&C 132:19).

Now to expect the Almighty God to share His limitless glory and the joys of exaltation without much effort on our parts is to cheapen His matchless plan of happiness. In order for celestial marriages to qualify for exaltation, husband and wife not only honor their covenants by sacrifice, but they also apply the principle of consecration in their most important relationships.

Sacrifice is *to give up*, but consecration is simply *to give*.[31] For missionaries, teachers, and parents, sacrifice becomes consecration when our actions are dedicated to bringing others unto the Savior. As spouses consecrate for each other—for the sole purpose of helping one another in their respective discipleships to the Savior—both are rewarded by gaining the individual and joint promises from their loving Heavenly Father. Only in this submission can spouses truly give their hearts to another and become afflicted in one another's afflictions (see D&C 30:6). In this special consecration, each spouse becomes a Christlike figure to the other, helping to carry burdens too heavy for the other to bear alone. "When we offer in our marriage a broken heart and a contrite spirit in similitude of the Good Shepherd, we promise to give our lives for the sheep of our covenant, a day or even an hour at a time. This process invites us to take selflessly upon ourselves both the afflictions and the joys of our companion and children, emulating in our own limited way how the Savior takes upon Himself our afflictions." Submission of both hearts thus produces "deep wellsprings of compassion"[32] and the rejoicings of a love that will endure throughout the eternities.

By consecrating our efforts to one another in celestial marriage, we will naturally consecrate ourselves to God and thus give our time and talent to bless our fellow man. As serious disciples of the Savior, our consecration incorporates the highest level of obedience—aligning our wills to God's will—with the highest level of sacrifice—yielding our whole souls to Him and His Father. Elder Neal A. Maxwell taught "if we really consecrate ourselves to Him, that consecrated self will be in the steady process of becoming like the Savior, attribute by attribute. This objective—knowing and becoming like the Master—is at the heart of King Benjamin's valedictory address." And so we can conclude that "only by aligning our wills with God's is full happiness to be found," for this "progression toward submission confers . . . an enhanced capacity for joy."[33]

Over the years, I have noticed that those who align their will to God are some of the most Christlike people I know. I do not doubt that they—especially those who are now single and deserve the richest joys of relationships—will be generously rewarded with exaltation as they persevere in rescuing others, all while enduring their own overwhelming and refining afflictions.

I testify that by the merits of Christ, the sacred relationship of husband and wife can be kept from falling into a telestial existence and can progress from a terrestrial marriage to a celestial and an eternal one. I testify that ordinances and covenants transform us and our marriages.

Except for the house of the Lord, there is no other place on earth where couples can make promises to become Christlike for each and then be given Christ's power to do so. We must return often to holy temples, and we must study the new and everlasting covenant of marriage as if our future depends on it. It does. Through this blessed covenant, we will discover the Savior's joy again and again. We will ever rejoice in the knowledge that His grace strengthens spouses to help one another fill the measure of their creations, become united as one, and receive exaltation with the Father and the Son. Truly, our greatest hopes are surrounded with the wondrous and joyous possibilities of living a consecrated life in mortality and then being crowned with a fulness of the Savior's joy in the hereafter.

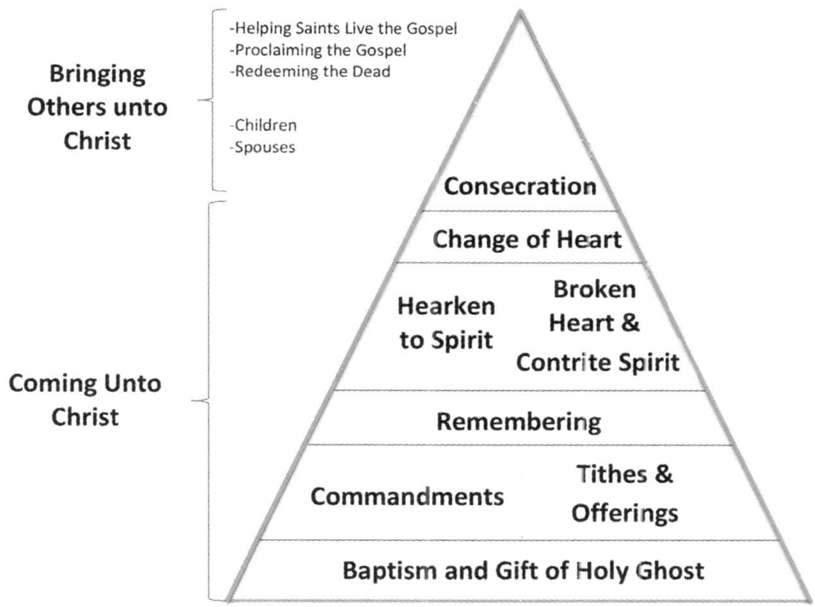

A SERIOUS (AND JOYOUS) DISCIPLE OF JESUS CHRIST

Notes

1. Spencer W. Kimball, "Oneness in Marriage," *Ensign,* March 1977.

2. Gary D. Chapman, Ph.D., *Things I Wish I'd Known Before We Got Married* (Chicago: Northfield Publishing, 2010), 9–10; see also Hugh W. Pinnock, "Making a Marriage Work," *Ensign,* September 1981.

3. Boyd K. Packer taught, "The ultimate purpose of the adversary . . . is to disrupt, disturb, and destroy the home and the family." ("The Father and the Family," *Ensign,* May 1994.)

4. Joseph B. Wirthlin, "Never Give Up," *Ensign,* November 1987.

5. Shayne M. Bowen, "Because I Live, Ye Shall Live Also," *Ensign,* November 2012.

6. Bruce R. McConkie, *A New Witness for the Articles of Faith* (Salt Lake City: Deseret Book, 1985), 24.

7. "The Family: A Proclamation to the World," *Ensign*, November 2010. Russell M. Nelson also taught that joy "is the gift that comes from intentionally trying to live a righteous life, as taught by Jesus Christ." ("Joy and Spiritual Survival," *Ensign*, November 2016.)

8. Gordon B. Hinckley, "Life's Obligations," *Ensign,* February 1999.

9. Jeffrey R. Holland, "The Laborers in the Vineyard," *Ensign,* May 2012; emphasis in original.

10. Russell M. Nelson, "Celestial Marriage," *Ensign,* November 2008.

11. Joseph Fielding Smith, *Doctrines of Salvation, Vol. II* (Salt Lake City: Bookcraft, 1955), 45–46.

12. Russell M. Nelson, "A Plea to My Sisters," *Ensign,* November 2015.

13. Margaret D. Nadauld, "The Joy of Womanhood," *Ensign,* November 2000.

14. Gordon B. Hinckley, "Rise Up, O Men of God," *Ensign,* November 2006.

15. Richard G. Ellsworth explains that in the Patriarchal Order of the Priesthood, men of God have the right "to preside over their descendants through all ages," and share in the ordinances and blessings of the priesthood with their wives "who are sealed [to them] in the temple. ("Priesthood," in Daniel H. Ludlow, ed., *Encyclopedia of Mormonism: The History, Scripture, and Procedure of The Church of Jesus Christ of Latter-day Saints,* vol.3 [New York: Macmillan, 1992], 3:1135.) See also

Boyd K. Packer, "What Every Elder Should Know—and Every Sister as Well: A Primer on Principles of Priesthood Government," *Ensign,* February 1993.

16. See Bruce R. McConkie, "Celestial Marriage" in *Mormon Doctrine* (Salt Lake City: Bookcraft, 1979), 84–85.
17. See www.lds.org/topics/kingdoms-of-glory?lang=eng; accessed 30 June 2017.
18. Russell M. Nelson, "Salvation and Exaltation," *Ensign,* May 2008.
19. See www.lds.org/topics/kingdoms-of-glory?lang=eng; accessed 30 June 2017.
20. See www.lds.org/manual/doctrine-and-covenants-student-manual /sections-132-138/section-132-marriage-an-eternal-covenant?lang =eng; accessed 3 July 2017.
21. Cree-L Kofford, "Marriage in the Lord's Way, Part One," *Ensign,* June 1998; emphasis in original.
22. Ibid.
23. Robert D. Hales, "A Little Heaven on Earth," *Ensign,* September 2011; emphasis in original.
24. Kofford, "Marriage in the Lord's Way, Part One"; emphasis in original.
25. D. Todd Christofferson, "As Many as I Love, I Rebuke and Chasten," *Ensign,* May 2011.
26. Tad R. Callister, *The Infinite Atonement* (Salt Lake City: Deseret Book, 2000), 221.
27. Cree-L Kofford, "Marriage in the Lord's Way, Part Two," *Ensign,* July 1998.
28. "Finding Rest in Christ," in *Teachings of Presidents of the Church: Joseph F. Smith* (2011), 424–32.
29. Elder Tad R. Callister taught, "To live with God does not assure us we will be like him. All who live in the celestial kingdom dwell with God, but only those who are exalted become as he is." (*The Infinite Atonement,* 26.)
30. See www.lds.org/scriptures/gs/holy-spirit-of-promise?lang=eng; accessed 3 July 2017.
31. Bruce C. Hafen and Marie K. Hafen, *The Contrite Spirit: How the Temple Helps Us Apply Christ's Atonement* (Salt Lake City: Deseret Book, 2015), 205.

32. Bruce C. Hafen, "The Temple and the Natural Order of Marriage," *Ensign,* September 2015.
33. Neal A. Maxwell, "King Benjamin's Manual of Discipleship," *Ensign,* January 1992; and Neal A. Maxwell, "Swallowed Up in the Will of the Father," *Ensign,* November 1995.

8: A Reason to Shout for *Joy*

In the premortal existence, we "shouted for joy" (Job 38:7) upon learning of God's promises to satisfy our deepest yearnings to be reunited with our Heavenly Parents and our mortal families. We were told we could live on this glorious earth, enjoy a physical body, and gain earthly experiences which would help us progress and gain eternal life.[1] Surely, we heard about the joys of agency and the sorrows accompanied with its misuse, as well as the wonders of our mortal bodies and the suffering associated with physical limitations and health challenges. Understanding intellectually what would and could happen, we happily accepted God's proposal.

With these preconceived ideas of mortality, however, it didn't take long before we experienced its "sobering realit[ies]" and began to "wonder what all the shouting was about."[2] Here, we often "see through a glass, darkly" (1 Corinthians 13:12), feeling "weighed down with sorrow, wading through much tribulation and anguish of soul" (Alma 8:14) because of the growing wickedness of the world. We don't remember our premortal life, and at times it is hard to envision the reality of the joys of our future.

At one particularly dark season of my life, trying to remember these promises was more than just challenging. After almost three years of the heartaches of infertility, my husband and I were excited to learn we would finally become parents. Our happiness was greatly subdued when an ultrasound detected the heart defect of our unborn child. Later a neonatologist told us that our baby's only hope of survival was a heart transplant. After twenty-four days of suffering in a newborn intensive care unit, our little Devin finished his mission on earth and died in my arms. The day we buried him, I thought my own heart would break. The process of healing was a long, demanding one, but the Savior strengthened me to carry the burden, He cleansed me of anger and resentment, He enabled me to forgive those who didn't understand my pain. Over time and through months and years of searching and reaching for the fruit of the Savior's Atonement, the Son of God completely mended my heart. Through His infinite grace and "the multitude of his tender mercies" (Ether 6:12), sadness turned to happiness, and joy returned to our lives.[3]

Not only did this experience reinforce our testimony of the majesty and love of Jesus Christ, but it also changed how we taught our other children about life after death. Over two decades after Devin's death, our family dinner led to a discussion about what it would be like to live in the celestial kingdom. When some of our children started musing about "sitting around playing harps" and other "boring stuff," my husband and I reminded them of the possibilities of being with their brother, Devin, again. I told them that because of the Savior's cleansing, strengthening, and healing power, my memories of Devin were sweet, and my thoughts of a glorious reunion with him brought immeasurable joy and excitement! I testified that he is near us and aware of our family's needs and that he has a keen interest in our joys.[4] We then emphasized that "the same sociality which exists among us here will exist among us there, only it will be coupled with eternal glory, which glory we do not now enjoy" (D&C 130:2). As we now appreciate spending time with those who help us stay true to our beliefs, so living in an exalted sphere with our righteous loved ones will be a most wonderful reward for following the Savior's perfect plan of happiness.

Through troubled times, we must not forget that the Savior's great "At-one-ment" was the reason we initially shouted for joy. And it is still the reason we should shout for joy on earth!

The word *Atonement* literally means "the bringing together of things that have been separated or estranged." Though physically and spiritually separated from God—and many of our loved ones—we rejoice in Christ's atoning sacrifice, which conquers death and hell and makes possible the joyous promise of the resurrection and redemption—or the bringing together of all souls who are estranged from God.[5] As we accept the conditions of the Savior's gospel and the promised blessings of His

Atonement, we come unto Christ, and then He returns us to Heavenly Father to be "at one" eternally.

Each of us will someday have the individual privilege of coming into the presence of the Savior and expressing our gratitude for His sacrifice. President Russell M. Nelson said:

> In a coming day you will present yourself before the Savior. You will be overwhelmed to the point of tears to be in His holy presence. You will struggle to find words to thank Him for paying for your sins, for forgiving you of any unkindness toward others, for healing you from the injuries and injustices of this life. You will thank him for strengthening you to do the impossible, for turning your weaknesses into strengths, and for making it possible for you to live with Him and your family forever.[6]

Elder Melvin J. Ballard likewise shared the joys of being in the presence of "the most glorious being . . . ever conceived":

> He smiled, called my name, and stretched out His hands towards me. . . . He put His arms around me and kissed me, as He took me into His bosom, and He blessed me until my whole being was thrilled. As He finished I fell at His feet, and there saw the marks of the nails; and as I kissed them, with deep joy swelling through my whole being, I felt that I was in heaven indeed. The feeling that came to my heart then was: Oh! If I could live worthy . . . so that in the end when I have finished I could go into His presence and receive the feeling that I *then* had in His presence, I would give everything that I am and ever hope to be![7]

Just as C. S. Lewis explained, true joy is not only the stabs we experience in mortality, but it is "an insatiable longing"[8] for future promises that are eternally linked to our past and present. We not only long to "[live] after the manner of happiness" (2 Nephi 5:27), but ultimately, we long to be reunited with our loved ones and our Heavenly Father and His Son. Truly, "our yearnings for happiness were implanted in our hearts by Deity. They represent a kind of homesickness, for we have a residual memory of our premortal existence. They are also a foretaste of the fulness of joy that is promised to the faithful." Because of Jesus Christ, "we can expect with perfect faith that our Father will fulfill our innermost longings for joy."[9]

Though the world defines joy as strong feelings of gladness and pleasure, real joy is what we experience on earth as we come unto Christ and become holy through our discipleship with Him. As we are willing to take His name upon us and follow Him, "much the same as an apprentice seeks to become like his or her master," we will "live so that the characteristics of Christ are woven into the fiber of [our] beings, as into a spiritual tapestry."[10] And, by keeping our covenants to our God and to our spouses, we become changed and purified through the merits of the Son of God, and we thereby gain at-one-ment with Them and a fulness of Their joy.

This joy—the Savior's joy—is within reach for all of us every day. Moroni promises: "*If* ye shall deny yourselves of all ungodliness, and love God with all *your* might, mind and strength, *then* is his grace sufficient for you that, by his grace ye may be perfect in Christ" (Moroni 10:32; emphasis added). What this means is that we can experience joy through Christ based on our individual capacity and "according to *our* works and the desires of *our* hearts."[11] "As we deny ourselves of ungodliness and honestly love God as fully as we are able, Christ's perfecting grace can complete the process of making us whole."[12]

Elder J. Devin Cornish declared that "Our Heavenly Father intends for us to make it! That is His work and His glory." Truly, "the God of heaven is not a heartless referee looking for any excuse to throw us out of the game. He is our perfectly loving Father, who yearns more than anything else to have all of His children come back home and live with Him as families forever." Our Heavenly Father wants us to have eternal life, and He sent His Son so that we could gain it![13]

Ultimately, discipleship is a choice, a choice that begins with desire. Eternal life is possible if we but want it, for those who long for a fulness of joy will be able "to enjoy that which they are willing to receive" (D&C 88:32). To gain the joys of coming unto Christ and becoming at-one with Him and His Father, we must be "filled with desire" (3 Nephi 19:24) and then act to find and keep the Savior's joy. Specifically, we must

- Desire the joys of a relationship with Heavenly Father. Obey His commandments and the promptings of His Spirit and then rejoice in His great love and the ongoing inspiration and purification of His Holy Spirit.

- Desire the joys of a discipleship with Christ. Sacrifice a broken heart and a contrite spirit through consistent repentance, good works, and submission to God's will, and thereby receive the cleansing, strengthening, and healing powers of Christ's Atonement.

- Desire the joys of enhanced relationships with others. Remember the goodness of God and the sacrifice of His Son through simple acts of faith, and delight in gaining the Christlike attributes of faith, knowledge, diligence, virtue, gratitude, hope, patience, and charity.

- Desire the joys of spiritual rebirth. Take upon the name of Christ through sacred ordinances, retain His name through keeping sacred covenants, and rejoice in sacred privileges to act in His name.

- Desire the joys of honoring covenants to bring others unto Christ. Help others live the gospel, proclaim His gospel to the world, and redeem the dead to experience the greatest joys of mortality.

- Desire the joys of a righteous posterity. Emulate the Father in establishing relationships with and teaching responsibility to children, and follow the Savior in honoring covenants by sacrifice to bring children unto Christ and help them become His disciples.

- Desire the joys of honoring the new and everlasting covenant or marriage. Sacrifice and consecrate time and efforts to spouses and to God and then discover the peace, fulfillment, and everlasting joys of celestial and eternal marriage.

Discipleship to the Savior is the prescribed pathway of joy. I testify that it is the only way to find and keep His joy. Elder Neal A. Maxwell said, "The taking of Jesus' yoke upon us constitutes serious discipleship. There is no greater calling, no greater challenge, and no greater source of joy—both proximate joy and ultimate joy—than that which is found in the process of discipleship. This process brings its own joys and reassurances."[14] President Russell M. Nelson thus exhorted us to "choose to be one of His true disciples now. Be one who truly loves Him, truly wants to serve and lead as He did."[15]

By accepting this challenge, I know we may all regularly shout for joy in the endless possibilities of the Savior's At-one-ment. Shout for joy whenever you see the hand of God in your life or whenever you recognize His goodness in the lives of those you love! Shout for joy whenever you receive Christ's tender mercies and whenever you experience His power to cleanse, strengthen, and heal you! Shout for joy whenever you feel the stirrings of the Holy Ghost and know the Savior's grace is working in your life! Shout for joy whenever you participate in priesthood ordinances and whenever you are strengthened to honor your covenants! Shout for joy whenever you surround yourself with loved ones and whenever you experience the joys of human friendships and enduring relationships! And shout for joy because you are given the chance to yield your heart unto Heavenly Father to gain the promises of salvation and exaltation by and through His Only Begotten Son!

I am eternally grateful for the joys I have experienced in mortality. I know we are here upon the earth to gain true joy, and I testify that we can find and keep the Savior's joy through relationships with God, our Eternal Father and with His Son, Jesus Christ. May we all experience joy in our journey by developing our own deep desires to draw near unto Christ and to lead others to the tree of life. I pray that we will recognize, partake, and cherish the "exceedingly great joy" (Mosiah 5:4) of the precious fruit of the Savior's Atonement—that which lifts, edifies, sustains, satisfies, and sweetens all along our pathway back Home.

Notes

1. "The Family: A Proclamation to the World," *Ensign*, November 2010.
2. Neal A. Maxwell, "Willing to Submit," *Ensign,* May 1985.
3. Fran C. Hafen, *Joy Cometh in the Morning: A Story of Healing from the Loss of a Child* (Salt Lake City: Desert Book, 2007).
4. President Joseph F. Smith taught: "Those who have been faithful, who have gone beyond . . . can see us better than we can see them; that they know us better than we know them.... We live in their presence, they see us, they are solicitous for our welfare, they love us now more than ever. For now they see the dangers that beset us; . . . their love for

us and their desire for our wellbeing must be greater than that which we feel for ourselves." (*Conference Report* [April 1916], 2–3.) See also Richard G. Scott, "How to Obtain Revelation and Inspiration for Your Personal Life," *Ensign,* May 2012.

5. See Jeffrey R. Holland, "The Atonement of Jesus Christ," *Ensign,* March 2008.
6. See Russell M. Nelson, in *Worldwide Devotional,* January 8, 2017, in www.lds.org/broadcasts/watch/worldwide-devotionals/2017/01?lang=eng&vid=5275057722001; accessed 10 January 2017.
7. Melvin R. Ballard, *Melvin J. Ballard: Crusader for Righteousness* (Salt Lake City: Bookcraft, 1966), 65–66, as quoted in Russell M. Ballard, "The Law of Sacrifice," *Ensign,* October 1998; emphasis in original.
8. See Colin Duriez, *Bedeviled: Lewis, Tolkien and the Shadow of Evil* (Westmont, Illinois: InterVarsity Press, 2015), 178.
9. Jack H. Goaslind, "Happiness," *Ensign,* May 1986.
10. Robert D. Hales, "Becoming a Disciple of Our Lord Jesus Christ," *Ensign,* May 2017.
11. "The Living Christ: The Testimony of the Apostles," *Ensign,* April 2000, 2; emphasis added.
12. Bruce C. Hafen, "The Temple and the Natural Order of Marriage," *Ensign,* September 2015.
13. J. Devin Cornish, "Am I Good Enough? Will I Make It?" *Ensign,* November 2016.
14. Neal A. Maxwell, "Becoming a Disciple," *Ensign,* June 1996.
15. See Nelson, in *Worldwide Devotional,* January 8, 2017, in www.lds.org/broadcasts/watch/worldwide-devotionals/2017/01?lang=eng&vid=5275057722001; accessed 10 January 2017.

Acknowledgments

I have often thought I should write a book about writing a book. It is a demanding, but sweetly satisfying journey. But it is a similar journey to the one each of us takes when we seek to learn truth. We have a question, and we are willing to believe that God knows the answer and will give it to us. We are also willing to do our part to search and to petition for heavenly help. When we are ready to receive revelation from God—which usually means after we have exhausted our resources—His Spirit adds light to our understanding. And then we marvel as the foundation of our knowledge swells with wondrous details and beautiful colors.

With my initial efforts of organizing my thoughts on joy, I knew I could only justify the time spent if it somehow benefited my family. The focus of the book therefore was directed to helping my children understand the true essence of joy. Not only would I talk with them about what I was learning, but I also outlined the chapters as letters to each of my living children. I started with an emphasis on obedience to my youngest daughter who was preparing for the ordinance of baptism and I ended with insights about the joys of marriage to my oldest daughter who was preparing to move away to college. Writing to my children gave me a chance to evaluate their unique developmental needs and to celebrate their spiritual successes. Eventually, the manuscript was adapted to anyone on the covenant path of discipleship.

I express my gratitude to the many people who have helped me in this endeavor. I am thankful for all those who allowed me to tell their stories and for Necia A. Clark who reviewed an earlier draft. I am grateful for the assistance of the Cedar Fort Publishing staff, especially McKell Parsons for getting me started; Kinsey Beckett for the beautiful cover design; and Deborah Spencer, Kaitlin Barwick, and Emily Chambers for their valuable edits and suggestions. I thank George Durrant for his generous foreword and his joyful way of life, as well as Tim Leavitt and Simon Dewey for their permission to use such a majestic image of the Savior.

Above all, I wish to recognize the support and encouragement of my husband, Dave, and my children, Emma, Claire, Lizzy, Anna, Michael, Abby and Wyatt Corbin, and Lauren and Cash Allred. I love you to the moon and back! Thanks for making a dream become a reality!

About the Author

FRAN C. HAFEN was born and raised in Lehi, Utah. She served a mission in Taiwan and earned her bachelor's and master's degrees from Brigham Young University. She enjoys writing family histories and recently compiled the missionary history of her former mission president (*The Morning Dew Awaits the Sun*). She is also the author of *Joy Cometh in the Morning: A Story of Healing from the Loss of a Child*. Fran and her husband, Dave, are the parents of eight children.

Scan to visit

www.franhafen.com